The Jesus Touch

A 12-week journey through the Gospels

with

Debbra Stephens

21st Century Christian Publishing

ISBN: 978-0-89098-696-7

Cover design by Jonathan Edelhuber

Dedication

Breezy & D ~

Jesus touched my life in many ways;

but the most cherished is

with you!

Boundless and eternal gratitude belongs

to my Gracious Lord

for leading me all the way on this incredible journey.

And I give special thanks to

Mike Sparks

Tom Tignor

Three of the dearest sisters:

Natalie Polutta, Jan Sessions, and Debbie Weaver

and the praying Elders and Staff of Burnt Hickory

TABLE OF CONTENTS

Anna, the Devoted

DAY 1

Our All-Seeing Lord

Dusk was settling on the outskirts of a Galilee fishing village. The needy gathered, bringing their illnesses, their burdens, their hurts…their hopes. Among the multitude, how easy to wonder their obscurity: "Am I just a blurred face lost in the crowd?"

Do you know that feeling?

You might if you have ever been to a popular sporting event that draws a crowd. In the crush of the stadium mass it's easy to feel like you might blend right into oblivion. Or maybe sitting alone, weighted down, you wonder if your need is overshadowed by all the others.

Then this verse is for you. Because Jesus is *for* **you**.

He. Sees. You.

Read Luke 4:40 in the sidebar and fill in the blank:

Jesus ______________________________ on each one.

Who did Jesus touch?

____

Luke 4:40

At sunset, the people brought to Jesus all who had various kinds of sickness, and laying his hands on each one, he healed them.

As He saw each one of them that historical Saturday in Capernaum, He sees you.

And Jesus touched each one.

His touch was not required for healing. Why, look at the verse just before this one.

Read Luke 4:39. How did Jesus heal Peter's mother-in-law?

The miracle of Jesus' healing was possible without touch. His touch was personal. It was a merciful, compassionate act. His touch was an expression of His heart... his love for the individual.

During our twelve weeks together we'll look at a select few to discover the unique touch Jesus had upon those He encountered. We will identify their need in order to answer two questions.

- Has Jesus touched me in a similar manner?
- Can I recognize that same need in someone around me so I can share that same sort of touch?

Jesus saw each face in the crowd. When we're out in public, do we notice the faces in the crowd? Or do we just see the crowd? Behind each face is a person. And each person may have a need that could use the Jesus touch.

TOUCHABILITY

Before we move forward in our study, let's briefly—and personally—consider this sense of touch.

Did you know that touch is the first sense humans develop?

TouchPoint

Your skin has approximately five million touch receptors. Each of your fingertips can have as many as 3,000.

We can experience touch in several ways, whereas our other senses are limited experientially. Your skin can experience touch by physical contact, change in pressure, or temperature. Studies have proven the importance of touch in helping to reduce anxiety, to aid in healing, in the powers of persuasion, and for healthy child development. Touch can reduce blood pressure and lower the heart rate. Touch releases endorphins that can actually reduce pain (see, kissing a boo-boo really works!). And touch provides calming reassurance.

But what of spiritual touch? What is the touchability of your faith? *Are you touchable*? Would you allow Jesus access to approach and affect every area of your life?

Won't you take a few moments to consider how Jesus touched you? In the space below record what it was you brought to Jesus for healing when you first met Him face-to-face:

____

____

Come to Jesus. He has THE touch all of us desperately need. And only He can touch your deepest need.

Now look up 2 Corinthians 1:3-4.

How are we meant to use God's comfort we have received?

____

____

It is by the loving compassion of our All-Seeing Lord, Jesus Christ, that we have received such great comfort. Mother Teresa of Calcutta issued this charge: "Let us touch the dying, the poor, the lonely and the unwanted according to the graces we have received and let us not be ashamed or slow to do the humble work."

My excitement of what lies before us has been building for some time now. I must say that I am overjoyed at the honor of our time together unveiling the Jesus Touch.

DAY 2

About Anna

Every church has them. Seasoned saints. They're the devout, dedicated, faithful servants of God.

It would seem the temple had them, too.

That's where we find our first profile. And what better place to start than with one touched by Jesus in His infancy? After all, He was making an impact on people's lives right from the start.

Let's look at Jesus' touch upon Anna.

Luke 2:36-38 describes her for us.

Match what you learn about her to her name.

	Jewess
	Married
Anna	**Devout**
	Rich
	Elderly

One of the things I love about Scripture is how you can glean so much from so little. Here we have two short verses, but they paint such a rich picture of dear Anna.

TouchPoint

The Bible makes reference to other prophetesses, such as; Philip's daughters (Acts 21:9); Miriam (Exodus 15:20); Deborah (Judges 4:4); Huldah (2Kings 22:14); and Isaiah's wife (Isaiah 8:3)

Anna, the prophetess, remained steadfast in prayer in the temple all of her widowed years.

Go back and re-read your text, and fill in the blanks:

"She never left the temple but worshiped

____________________ and ____________________.

What would that look like in your life if you worshiped night and day?

____

____

And her faithfulness was rewarded when she met the Messiah for whom she had watched and waited.

AVAILABILITY

I would think that spending the better part of 60 years in the temple she learned a few things about the prophecies of God's Promised Messiah. And she would have come to know the Law of Moses enough to know about the purification requirements for a firstborn son. Anna made herself available. She was strategically placed so that when the time had come, her long-awaited Hope was fully realized.

How did she respond to this encounter?

☐ **Walked away, untouched**

☐ **Gave thanks to God**

☐ **Spoke of Him to others**

☐ **She scolded Simeon for his praise**

We read in the text that Anna gave thanks to God and spoke of this Blessed Child to all who were "looking forward to the redemption of Israel."

And isn't that just what the devoted and spiritually disciplined of God do? Look forward? Isn't that what hope does?

What do you suppose she prayed for "night and day"? She knew the state of her nation and the afflictions of her people. And she knew God's promise for the coming salvation Simeon spoke of. So how do you suppose Jesus touched her?

Spiritually. She realized an answer to both her prayers and her hope. Her faith was rewarded when she witnessed God's promise fulfilled.

Has Jesus ever touched you spiritually?
Share your experience:

____

____

What was your response when He did?

____

____

There is nothing more exhilarating than when Jesus touches you spiritually through answered prayer. He has graciously rewarded my faith and energized my hope time and again with each answer to prayer. And when He does, I cannot contain my thanksgiving! Nor can I keep from sharing with others what He has done.

Anna exercised her faith and kept her hope alive so that in her waiting, she prepared. She was ready to receive her Lord when He finally arrived. But in order to recognize Him when He came, she had to be watching and ready.

Tomorrow we'll look closely at what our waiting should look like.

DAY 3

What Waiting Does

I can remember just a few short years back when I found myself in a season of waiting. I had gotten laid-off from work and it seemed like I was waiting on everything—mostly communication. I waited for appointments by e-mail, unemployment checks by postal mail, interview opportunities by phone ... and answered prayer.

Most of us find ourselves waiting. Waiting for change. So, the better question is not if you're waiting, but what you're waiting for.

Consider what you might be waiting on in this season of your life:

- ☐ **Career change**
- ☐ **Finances**
- ☐ **Results**
- ☐ **Improved health**
- ☐ **Relationship**
- ☐ **Good news**

How do you find yourself responding in the wait?

- ☐ **Busy**
- ☐ **Distracted**
- ☐ **Discouraged**
- ☐ **Worried**
- ☐ **Confident**
- ☐ **Hopeful**

Would we not find greater contentment waiting on God? Not waiting for His blessing ... but Him. Not waiting for Him to do something ... but waiting before Him.

Waiting asks much of us. It requires patience. It requires trust. And it requires disciplined activity.

WAITING HOPES

Anna knew what she was waiting for ... and Who she was waiting on. Her wait did not disappoint—for her wait was steeped in hope ... and hope in God never disappoints.

The prophet Jeremiah wrote; "The Lord is good to those who wait for him, to the soul who seeks him" (Lamentations 3:25). And Isaiah said that those "who wait for the Lord shall renew their strength; they shall mount up with wings like eagles; they shall run and not be weary; they shall walk and not faint" (Isaiah 40:31). How often in her many years did God renew Anna's strength? How she must have trusted His goodness to endure the oppression of Rome and the religious authorities. And how often her hope in these words must have helped her in her wait.

Psalm 130:5

I wait for the Lord,
my whole being waits,
and in his word I put
my hope.

Consider Psalm 130:5 in the sidebar.
Where did the psalmist place his hope?

Hope in God's Word never disappoints, for it is reliable and unerring. Filling our minds with the truth of God's Word lends the assurance our faith needs to keep hope strong: the hope that feeds our wait.

The day Jesus touched Anna, He touched another temple regular... also waiting.

Read Luke 2:25-32. Who is mentioned in this passage?

Circle all that apply to Simeon from what you read:

Righteous and devout
Young
Waiting
Lacking the Holy Spirit
Knowledge of God's Word

Simeon had been waiting to see the Lord's Christ. In his waiting, he trusted God and His promise to him. His encounter with Jesus sparked praise and rejoicing, to witness the coming of the salvation of the Lord.

Now let's look at Isaiah 30:18 and fill in the blank:

Blessed are ______________________ who wait for him!

Are just some blessed who wait on God?______________

Are just the perfect blessed who wait on God?_________

Are only the achievers blessed that wait on God? ______

All who wait on God are blessed. Isn't it the time spent with Him in the waiting that's the greater blessing? Setting our minds on Him in stillness and rest, dear one, is what helps us remain diligent in our faith—all the while adding patience to our endurance.

I've got one more uplifting verse for you today.

Read Psalm 27:14 in the sidebar.
How can we wait for the Lord?

____

Psalm 27:14

Wait for the Lord;
be strong and
take heart and
wait for the Lord.

While we wait, we can remain strong and take heart. By trusting God, having hope in His unfailing Word, as we have already seen, our hearts can have courage. But there is one more key, another necessary practice that Anna and Simeon shared of which the New Testament speaks often.

Watching.

WAITING WATCHES AND READIES

If you were to do a Bible search on the word *watch* in the New Testament alone, you would be amazed at the results. A state of watchfulness is mentioned numerous times with regard to our faith by the Gospel and epistle writers alike.

Read our Lord's words recorded in Matthew 24:42.
What are we to do and why?

____

____

Watchmen would anticipate morning, when the dark cover for the prowling enemy had passed and they were most prone to attack. Do we heed the Lord's warning with this same commitment as watchmen?

Psalm 130:6

I wait for the Lord
more than watchmen
wait for the morning,
more than watchmen
wait for the morning.

Luke 12:40 reads: "You also must be ready, because the Son of Man will come at an hour when you do not expect him."

We must also be ______________________________ .

Jesus teaches that we must remain both watchful and ready, as did Anna. Someday we, too, will see our Savior.

Do we live with that same expectation as Anna and Simeon?
Next, we'll see just how we can make ready.

DAY 4

Making Ready

Our family loves to camp. I grew up camping, and I started taking my kids when they were young. But there is one thing about camping (especially with a family); it takes planning and preparation. I saved packing lists on my computer and, over time, I stocked storage tubs with the necessary gadgets and gear so that we would always be ready. At a moment's notice, I could have the car loaded and ready to roll.

We do well when we take the same care in matters of the soul. We've seen how watching and waiting are important. But being ready is of utmost importance.

So how does one make ready?

I love Peter's instruction in this regard. Turn to 1 Peter 1:13 in your Bible and then read the NRSV I've copied below for comparison:

> **"Therefore prepare your minds for action; discipline yourselves; set all your hope on the grace that Jesus Christ will bring you when he is revealed."**

List Peter's three instructions:

1) ____

2) ____

3) ____

In order to prepare our minds and keep hope alive, we must live spiritually disciplined lives.

Libraries and Christian bookstores are filled with helpful resources in the practice of spiritual disciplines. But, using Anna as our model, the text says she remained "faith-full" simply through worship, prayer, and fasting. I am all for spiritual disciplines and have trained in several over the years (we'll get to more about that in a minute). But through the grace of God that comes by faith and the powerful working of the Holy Spirit, we can train in readiness armed with our Bibles, with bowed heads and bent knees, and a committed desire to seek after God's will.

SPIRITUAL DISCIPLINES SIMPLIFIED

Practices of spiritual disciplines are as varied as church traditions. Volumes can be, and have been, written on the matter (that is not my intent here). But the underlying factor is a matter of the heart.

TouchPoint

"The true heart of spiritual discipline is a relationship with God." Barbara Hughes, *Disciplines of a Godly Woman*

What has your experience been in this area?

____

What spiritual disciplines have made the biggest impact on your spiritual maturity?

____

I'm sure I'm not telling you anything new when I say that the key is time spent with God. Intentional, diligent, and consistent time in prayer and Bible study is the most effective training to be had. By them we remain in close fellowship with Jesus—making ourselves accessible ... and touchable.

I cannot possibly over-stress the crucial necessity of time spent delving the depths of God's Word. And I'll point back to Anna. I can't help but imagine that she was well-versed in the Law and the Prophets. She must have known the Scriptures—that a child would be born and would have to be brought to the temple according to the Law. She lived her life near to God, and should the timing of the coming Savior eclipse her generation, she was not going to miss it.

Knowing the Word is to know what you're watching and waiting for.

But I would be remiss to leave us there. We have to take this full-circle. So turn to James 1:22 and complete the command:

We can't just read God's Word, we must:

A B C D (Circle one)

____

Time spent in His Word is time spent hearing His voice and learning His will ... *in order to do what it says.*

I know there are many Annas out there, or you wouldn't be holding this study in your dear hands. As you know, it's good practice to review and renew your level of commitment from time-to-time. So before we move on from this place, take the time to evaluate your current spiritual condition. Make a renewed commitment to establish a consistent and realistic routine, to set aside time daily in communion with your Heavenly Father and Lord Jesus Christ. Reach out to another sister-in-the-faith to share this and for encouragement and accountability.

How will you choose to follow Peter's instruction in our key verse above?

___

And finally, sister, above all; heed the words of Paul to the Corinthians—remember grace.

> **"But by the grace of God I am what I am, and his grace to me was not without effect. No, I worked harder than all of them—yet not I, but the grace of God that was with me" (1 Corinthians 15:10).**

DAY 5

Sharing the Touch

I don't know about you, but Anna has become near and dear to my heart. Anna worshiped ... and watched ... and waited—in faith, hope, and trust. How impressed I am with her steadfast faith in turbulent and difficult times! She persevered faithfully, regardless of her circumstances.

God honored Anna by turning faith to sight. And how thankful I am that she experienced the touch of Jesus in such a real and significant way—spiritually. Jesus answered her prayers and rewarded her for her devoted waiting.

Can you name any Annas among you? Do you know of any faithful, elderly servants of God who have endured the trials of this life?

There is bound to be someone that could use the encouraging touch their hope needs. It's a matter of training ourselves to notice them in the crowd and putting our spiritual training into action.

That Jesus-touch is yours to share by encouraging the watching and waiting.

How can you share that same touch with the person you named above?

____

____

THE BLESSING IN BLESSING

And in the grand economy of God, He undoubtedly blesses those who choose to bless others. We can learn much and be encouraged by the spiritual mentors God places among us. I urge you to seek them out, to learn from and to serve.

Let's look briefly at Mary.

Read Luke 1:39 in the sidebar and complete the sentence:

Mary arose and went with______________________ .

Luke 1:39

In those days Mary arose and went with haste into the hill country, to a town in Judah, and she entered the house of Zechariah and greeted Elizabeth.

After being visited by Gabriel with news of her Divine conception, she hurried to Elizabeth, a woman in her "old age," who could empathize her plight. They were able to share their God-experience in support of each other.

That phone call I mentioned earlier in this lesson, waiting for a job? I was blessed when it finally came from the owner of an assisted living facility. I am encouraged in my faith daily by those who have endured some of the harshest trials of life and remain joyful in hope. Many of them experience an assortment of difficulties that come with increased age, but they remain unwavering in their faith. When my spirit needs a boost, God can be counted on to use them to lift me up (when I'm the one trying to encourage them).

I hope you have seen this week that we must remain like Anna—in a state of watchful readiness. And, I dare say, we have come to a point at which we can answer the following question without hesitation: "Can't we share the touch of Jesus with others doing the same?"

Let's close our week together in prayer, that our response will be the same as hers. (Go back and look up Luke 2:38 and fill in the blanks.)

That we will give______ to God and speak about

Jesus________________ ____________ who are

looking______________ to the redemption of Jerusalem.

WEEK TWO

John, the Persecuted

DAY 1

From Glory to Gloom

John, the ... *what* ?!

At first glance of our title this week, you're likely to think one of two things: 1) "I must be thinking of a different John," or 2) "She's crazy!"

Yes, I'm referring to John, the Baptist. Hang in there and you'll see where his days of glory soon turned to gloom.

As sure as the promised Coming Messiah, His messenger, too, was prophesied.

Read Malachi 3:1:

John was called God's ______________________________

Read Isaiah 40:3:

He would ____

ABOUT JOHN

John was a miracle-child promised by angels and whose birth was foretold by prophets. What can we deduce of him?

Read Luke 1:15-17 and fill in the blanks:

- **He would be** ______________________ **before the Lord.**
- **He would be** __________________ **with the Holy Spirit.**

"This all happened at Bethany on the other side of the Jordan, where John was baptizing."

John 1:28

Read Matthew 3:1-12. Circle all that apply:

He was mild.	**He was passionate.**
He was bold.	**He spoke a soft message.**
He was eccentric.	**He drew great crowds.**

Read Luke 3:1-18 John was teaching and preaching (check all that apply):

- ☐ **Repentance/Baptism**
- ☐ **Exemption of Abraham's descendants**
- ☐ **Coming of the Messiah**
- ☐ **Ethics**
- ☐ **Future judgment**

He left his family and comforts of home to preach repentance and the coming kingdom of God—paving the way for the baptism of the Christ.

John, though a servant of God like Anna from last week's lesson, he is at the polar opposite end of the personality spectrum. He was loud, bold, uncompromising and zealous for the Lord. But the crowds swarmed about him.

He challenged authorities corrupting religion and never backed-down from rulers that behaved unethically. Let's see what happens when your firmly stated beliefs ruffle the governor's royal feathers.

Complete Luke 3:19-20:

But when John ________________ Herod the tetrarch because of his marriage to Herodias, his brother's wife, and all the other evil things he had done, Herod added this to them all:

____

He courageously confronted Herod Antipas, condemning his relationship with Philip's wife. Antipas had divorced his wife in order to marry Herodias—who not only was married to his brother, but was also his niece.

TouchPoint

Herod Antipas, Tetrarch of Galilee, was the ruling governor appointed by Rome and son of Herod the Great.

Would you so boldly confront someone's sin?

____

Can you remember a time you challenged blatant sin?

____

____

As a result, Herod had John tossed in prison.

DAY 2

The Quieted Herald

"It was the best of times, it was the worst of times, it was the age of wisdom, it was the age of foolishness, it was the epoch of belief, it was the epoch of incredulity, it was the season of Light, it was the season of Darkness, it was the spring of hope, it was the winter of despair." Although A Tale of Two Cities was penned by Charles Dickens in 1859, it more aptly suited the times of John. They were the best of times because the long-awaited Messiah had arrived on the scene. It was the worst because of the oppression by religion and government alike. They had the wisdom of John, but the foolishness of the Pharisees. There reigned faith and skepticism, light and darkness, hope ... and despair.

Day Two with John finds this quieted herald sitting in Herod's jail cell for speaking his righteous convictions.

We don't know how long he was there, how he was treated, or the condition of his confinement, but have you ever considered the real possibility that he got discouraged?

I believe it is here that we can sense a noticeable shift in John's tone and disposition.

What do you "hear" when you read Luke 7:18-19?

____

____

Do you hear duress? Discouragement? Possibly even despair?

Has standing up for what is right ever landed you in a lonely place?

____

WHAT IN THE WORLD DOES THE WORLD DO WITH A PROPHET?

John wouldn't be the first prophet to have cause for despair. I'm sure he knew the history of Elijah's persecution at the hands of Jezebel. (Especially since he was often compared to him!) Jeremiah, another famous prophet, was persecuted at the hands of his own King Zedekiah.

Read Jeremiah 37 and document the treatment Jeremiah received from King Zedekiah.

____

____

____

Jeremiah was imprisoned and eventually charged with treason for his message about Babylon's capture of Jerusalem.

TouchPoint

Tradition says that Isaiah, yet another of God's messengers, was charged with falsely predicting the destruction of Judah and executed at the hands of Manasseh.

Martyrdom and Ascension of Isaiah

Recorded in Matthew 23:37 are the convicting words of Jesus: (fill in the blanks):

"Jerusalem, Jerusalem, you who ____________________ the prophets and _______________ those sent to you"

Considering all this, how easy would it have been for John to doubt? I imagine his understanding of how things should be going, compared to the circumstances in which he found himself, just didn't match up.

I have found myself in painful situations when reality just didn't align with my worldview. A worldview that screams; "If I'm doing God's will, I will always be treated fairly."

Can you relate? Have you ever stood firm on biblical principle and suffered consequences that didn't align with your expectations?

____

____

____

If John was doing the will of God, which he believed he was, it doesn't seem a far stretch to think he wondered, *Why am I imprisoned*?

TELL ME AGAIN

The same man who proclaimed unequivocally; "I have seen and I testify that this is God's Chosen One," was seeking confirmation. He sought reassurance.

Read Luke 7:19 in the sidebar. Star the matching quotes:

You are the one who is to come . . .

Are you the one who is to come . . .

We shouldn't expect anyone else . . .

Should we expect someone else . . .

Luke 7:19

John sent them to the Lord to ask, "Are you the one who is to come, or should we expect someone else?"

I hear in John's question; "Tell me again . . ." that he needed a reminder.

Trials seem to first assault our memories—clouding our knowledge, muddling our faith, and inflicting amnesia of who we know Jesus to be. I become most fearful when I have forgotten that God is sovereign, mighty, and good. It is precisely then that it is wise to follow in John's stead and prayerfully ask Jesus for a reminder.

Have you been or are you now in the midst of a situation in which you need to remember Who Jesus Is?

____

____

____

DAY 3

A Reassuring Touch

The Bible Camp my kids have attended for years is situated on one of the most heavenly pieces of earth. It is scenic, serene and spectacular. But it is isolated. When they go in, no communication comes out until they come home a week later.

I can honestly say I have never worried about them while they were there, but it was always nice to hear they were OK. A few years back, our Children's Minister went to spend the day. It was a welcome message when she told me all was well. I felt my heart instantly settle—touched by a reassuring word.

John asked. And Jesus answered. Jesus honored this suffering servant's request by sending back a powerful reminder.

Jesus replied, "Go back and report to John what you hear and see: The blind receive sight, the lame walk, those who have leprosy are cleansed, the deaf hear, the dead are raised, and the good news is proclaimed to the poor."
Matthew 11:4-6

Jesus knew just what John needed most—reassurance. So Jesus touched this prophet and preacher with a familiar word he would recognize.

Jesus instructed the messengers to report what

"you____________ and __________________"

AN EVIDENT MESSIAH

By testifying to what they saw and heard, these messengers were affirming proof-positive evidence. The Messiah whom John was heralding would perform specific deeds as evidence of sure identity.

Match the verse of promise with the affliction:

Blind	**Isaiah 35:6**
Lame	**Isaiah 61:1**
Deaf	**Isaiah 26:19**
Dead	**Isaiah 29:18**
Poor	**Isaiah 35:5**

As a fellow-prophet, John would recognize the expected deeds of the promised Messiah foretold by preceding prophets. Jesus reassured John with the fact that He was filling the shoes only the Messiah could fill.

This reminder helped John to see more clearly what God was doing in accordance with what He had promised. The Messiah of God may not always do what we expect, but He will always do as God has promised.

In the face of adversity, what is it you quickly forget about the Christ of God?

____

____

How important is it to remember what He has said . . . what He has done?

____

____

Read Psalm 42:6. What did the Sons of Korah say to do when souls are downcast?

____

A MESSIAH AND HIS MIRACLES

Jesus openly performed the miraculous as display of God's divine power, His authority and proof of His identity in fulfilling prophecy.

Look up Acts 2:22 and fill in the blank:

"Fellow Israelites, listen to this: Jesus of Nazareth was a man ______________________________ by God to you by miracles, wonders and signs, which God did among you through him, as you yourselves know."

Jesus exercised His authority through the signs, wonders, and miracles He performed. He testified: "All authority in heaven and on earth has been given to me (Matt 28:18).

TouchPoint

Apodeiknumi = accredited: to *demonstrate, set forth, exhibit, attest, approve. Thayers Greek Lexicon* states; "The ancient Greek philosophers used this term for 'putting forth certain proof."

Abbott-Smith

Write the letter of the realm of Jesus' authority next to the miracle.

________	**Calm the sea**	**A) Death**
________	**Forgive**	**B) Illness**
________	**Heal the lame**	**C) Nature**
________	**Raise the dead**	**D) Demons**
________	**Cast out evil spirits**	**E) Sins**

THE WONDER IN ALL THESE WONDERS

Jesus declared His authority time and again. Multitudes, however—both then and now—have stumbled over it. It is a wonder, that in all His wonders, people wonder still.

TouchPoint

Skandalizó = stumble: to put a snare, to cause to sin, to give offense.

Strong's

Read Matthew 11:6.

What did Jesus say of the one who does not stumble because of Him?

____

Blessed are those who do not fall away because they become ensnared or offended on account of Jesus.

There is nothing more reassuring than truth. In times of difficulty, it is easy to become blinded to truth. Jesus touched John with reassuring, reaffirming truth. The truth of His authority. And the truth of His identity by the truth of His activity.

Jesus' response to John is an encouragement to all believers who have asked that same question since. Jesus did not berate or belittle, but gently guided him to the truth his heart most needed. The lesson to be learned for us all is not to allow our senses to overtake what we know to be true. Trust what you see ... not what you feel.

DAY 4

A Heart Divided

So far, we have seen John blanket the gamut of the human landscape. He scaled the heights—experiencing the success of a thriving, vibrant ministry; and trudged the depths—wondering if his suffering in prison bore merit.

When we look more closely at Jesus' response, we get a sense that there is more going on than meets the eye. Jesus did more by quoting Scripture than soothe John's bout with doubt. He did what only Jesus can—He strengthened his faith.

I don't know about you, friend, but my heart and my mind, at times, are impossibly inseparable! It's as if they're one giant organ ... with my heart being the dominant dictator.

Things get out-of-whack when my heart and mind are unbalanced. Either I over-analyze a situation or react emotionally. Neither extreme is particularly effective.

Why?

Faith becomes divided.

KNOWING vs. FEELING

Picture your faith as a heart made up of knowledge (what you believe) and emotions (what you feel). Think of it as head-faith (what you know) and heart-faith (what you feel)

When heart-faith overtakes head-faith—when what you feel overpowers what you know—remember what you believe.

When one overrules the other, your heart can become divided, often lopsided.

As with John, his heart-faith (his feelings) had taken over. So Jesus addressed his head-faith.

Read Matthew 11:4.

Jesus said;

"Tell John what you ____________ and ____________."

Jesus recalibrated John's heart back into balance. He helped him remember what he believed. He helped shift the focus of John's faith from what he felt to what he knew.

Have you ever been in a similar position? Have you found yourself alone in a dark place when your feelings overtook what you knew to be true?

____

____

____

Read Psalm 55:22.

What are we told to do?

____

1 Peter 5:7

Cast all your anxiety on him because he cares for you.

Read the verse in the sidebar. Why should you cast your cares on Jesus?

____

Do you know someone now in a vulnerable position who needs the same reminder?

____

____

____

Read Isaiah 35:3-4.

What can you tell them?

____

We all reach a crisis of faith at some point in time. They are defining moments that can strengthen and refine our faith. But only when we turn to the One who recalibrates our faith, is it put back into proper balance.

Do what John did. Turn to Jesus. Seek the reassurance your faith needs by looking to Him.

Jesus graced John with the truth of His Word to answer his heart-faith questions. Do the same. Turn to passages like Isaiah 50:10:

> "Who among you fears the LORD
> and obeys the word of his servant?
> Let the one who walks in the dark,
> who has no light,
> trust in the name of the LORD
> and rely on their God."

And believe.

DAY 5
Touching the Persecuted

It began with Cain and Abel. It happens in the media, in our schools, in our homes, even—and especially—in religion.

Persecution.

Stephen testified before the Sanhedrin to its existence from centuries past:

> "Was there ever a prophet your ancestors did not persecute? They even killed those who predicted the coming of the Righteous One. And now you have betrayed and murdered him" (Acts 7:52).

From the prophets, to the Author of our faith, Jesus Christ, all were persecuted for their faith. The first followers of Jesus were not immune either. Stephen was the first martyred for his beliefs. And tradition says that eleven of the twelve apostles also died a martyrs' death.

And it is as much alive today as it has ever been.

A report conducted by China Aid stated that there was a 372% increase in incidents of persecution in China in 2012 over 2006. This has been attributed to, in part, the 2012 Chinese Communist government's plan to eliminate all unregistered house churches.

And there are reports regularly in the news, like the one featured in the sidebar that occurred in September 2013.

TouchPoint

Peshawar, Pakistan—Suicide bombers detonate amid Christians worshipping on Sunday at All Saints Church—killing 85, wounding 140. "Christians have often been attacked by Sunni Muslim militants, who view them as enemies of Islam because of their faith."

Associated Press, published by *Fox News*

THE MASTER'S TEACHING

Prior to sending out the 12 apostles, Jesus gave explicit instructions (Matthew 10:5-42). He also told them; "I am sending you out like sheep among wolves."

Match up His additional warnings of treatment they might expect from Matthew 10:

_______ **Verse 17** **A) Betrayed**

_______ **Verse 19** **B) Arrested**

_______ **Verse 21** **C) Persecuted**

_______ **Verse 22** **D) Flogged**

_______ **Verse 23** **E) Hated**

Daunting ... to say the least! But within the overarching passage is encouragement and promise—the mightiest of which is found is verse 28: "Do not be afraid of those who kill the body but cannot kill the soul. "

On the night of his arrest Jesus spoke at length to the apostles of this expected phenomenon.

Read John 15:18-25. Complete verse 18:

"If the world________________ ____________________,

keep in mind that it_________ _________ _________."

What explanation did Jesus give for the hatred toward them in verse 19?

____

In verse 20 Jesus said, "If they persecuted me, they will persecute you also." Circle the reason:

A servant is greater than the master.

A servant is not greater than his master.

A master is not greater than his servant.

Jesus knows full-well the propensity for evil in man's wicked heart. He forewarned the apostles of the troubles to come and tried to prepare them as much as was possible. His dialogue continues on into chapter 16 of John's Gospel:

> "All this I have told you so that you will not fall away. They will put you out of the synagogue; in fact, the time is coming when anyone who kills you will think they are offering a service to God. They will do such things because they have not known the Father or me. I have told you this, so that when their time comes you will remember that I warned you about them." (1-4)

Jesus was not only their example, but their encouragement.

Read John 16:33.

Why did Jesus tell them all these things?

____

____

____

Jesus assured them that in this world

they would have________________ .

What is our blessed hope?

____

This is not meant to be a study of the individuals as much as it is their encounter with Jesus. By that we can draw out the need Jesus met so that we can become aware of that same need in others in order to touch them in a similar manner.

By this encounter with John, we see that Jesus touched this persecuted servant with encouragement and reassurance—a real need around the globe today.

We can be informed and moved to act in support and encouragement of missionaries imprisoned in dangerous parts of the world. We can reach out and touch them with God's reaffirming Word, strengthening their faith under fire. And we can definitely—and most importantly—"pray on all occasions."

TouchPoint

Websites of Note:

PrayforthePersecuted.com

Persecution.org

OpenDoorsUSA.org

PrisonAlert.com

ChristiansinCrises.net

GFA.org/persecution

ChinaAid.org

John lived differently, set apart from the world. He lived what he preached. And he went out into the wilderness to prepare the way for others to know Jesus. While serving the Lord, he was imprisoned for his message and ultimately lost his life (Matthew 14:3-13). But when he reached a low point being persecuted for his faith—Jesus touched him with a reassuring word.

So can we.

WEEK THREE

Philip, the Useful

DAY 1

First Contact

Let's just say that today was going to be the most important day of your life.

Wouldn't you prepare for it?

My daughter's recent graduation comes to mind. A lot of planning and preparation went into that day. They practiced for days, rehearsing every cue. She had her clothes laid out, her bags packed, and her alarm set well in advance.

Excitement charged the air.

I recall my wedding day and my baby-birthing days—all significant, life-changing days.

What about those you didn't know to plan for? The days that caught you by surprise?

Such was the case for Philip.

THE EARLY DAYS

But let's turn the clock back a couple days before Philip met Jesus, in order to set the scene. We'll retrace Jesus' steps to get a bearing on the context of His first encounter with Philip. Let's start with John 1:35 and dig for details: "The next day John was there again with two of his disciples."

According to John 1:19-27, this is John, _______________ .

The location is found in John 1:28:

So we discover that John, the Baptist is in Bethany with two men. This Bethany is not to be confused with the Bethany near Jerusalem, the hometown of Lazarus, Mary and Martha. This Bethany is near the Jordan River—its exact whereabouts is now undetermined. As for the men, let's see what we can find about them.

TouchPoint

Although Philip was a Hellinistic Jew, he is always referred to by his Greek name, Philip. Most would have had both a Greek name and a Jewish name. Philip's Jewish name is never mentioned.

Look at John 1:37-40 to uncover one identity:

Most scholars agree that the second man is John, the apostle. Most of the time when referring to himself in the first person in his Gospel, he doesn't use his name.

Now let's see if we can get an idea about timing. Consider John 1:32-34 and answer the following question:

"I have seen and I testify that this is God's Chosen One."
John 1:34

What major event is John testifying to that seems to have already taken place?

It seems that Andrew and John were following John, the Baptist in Bethany when he pointed to Jesus and testified that Jesus was the "Lamb of God." Andrew and John "spent the day with Jesus." And the first thing Andrew did was to go tell his brother Simon, "We have found the Messiah."

Using John 1:43, fill in the following blanks:

When: ______________________________

Where: ______________________________

What: ______________________________

Who: ______________________________

The text tells us Jesus leaves for Galilee the next day and finds Philip. Now we don't know exactly where in Galilee. We do know, however, that Philip is from Bethsaida.

According to John 1:44, who else is from Bethsaida?

Philip, Andrew, and Peter, and likely Nathanael, were all fishermen from Bethsaida. Lifetime friends. And they most likely attended the same synagogue together, which explains Philip's reference to the prophets and the law of Moses (John 1:45).

On this one exceptional day, early in Jesus' ministry, we see his first encounter with Philip. And Jesus had but two words for Philip:

____________________ ____________________

TouchPoint

John records more details about Philip than any other Gospel writer.

Two words: "Follow me." But following isn't always easy, is it? I used those words with my kids when we would hike the trails. It seemed a simple enough request. I would grin when they would veer off course, lag behind, or speed up ahead.

And Philip's response? It was classic! Authentic. One he knew not to prepare for. He runs—eager with excitement—to tell a friend, "We have found him."

This signifies two things:

1. He believed what the Scriptures taught him.
2. He was seeking the Messiah.

When Jesus found you, were you seeking?

Did you believe He was what the Scriptures say about Him?

With what things might you still struggle?

____

____

____

There was no way for Philip to know that his life would be forever changed on that particular day. Maybe it's better that he didn't know. It might not have gone quite so well, considering our human tendency to try to manipulate certain outcomes.

Philip met Jesus. He believed. He shared. There was nothing more that planning and preparing could have accomplished to perfect the day.

DAY 2

Touching Encounters

It's early spring in Bethsaida—near Passover. From their lofty perch atop the mountain, they see multitudes gathering below. Jesus knows the needs of the crowd assembling before Him. And He knows the needs of His apostles-in-training at His side.

First, let's determine the reason the crowd is following Jesus by reading John 6:1-4:

Not wanting a teaching opportunity to pass, Jesus turns specifically to Philip with the following question:

Complete Jesus' question to Philip from John 6:5:

"________________ shall we ____________ bread

for these people to eat?"

Some commentaries allude to the fact that Philip's role among the troupe was provisions (much like Judas was given the responsibilities of treasurer). Or maybe Jesus posed this particular question to Philip because he was from Bethsaida and would be familiar with the area. Both possible. Both valid. But I believe the real reason Jesus directed this question to Philip is already given for us.

John 6:6

He asked this only to test him, for he already had in mind what he was going to do.

Look at John 6:6 in the sidebar and give the answer stated:

____

Jesus intended to test his faith (as well as all those present) by means of a simple question. The touch of Jesus is always a matter of faith.

The encounter is brief... but powerful. A simple question... packed with purpose. And we see Jesus touch Philip's personality.

PRACTICALLY MINDED

Consider that Philip's response came from his natural inclination. He made a practical response to refute just how impractical Jesus' question was. Philip looked out over the crowd and calculated cost. Overwhelmed by what seemed to be an impossibility, he responded instinctively and logically.

Look at Jesus' question again. Notice he asked Philip "where." But Philip answered (in verse 7) "how."

By basically saying it couldn't be done, he was limiting Jesus' ability to provide.

How easy is that?!

More times than I care to admit, I have been in an overwhelming situation and assessed it "impossible!" All the while denying the infinite possibility of Jesus.

Can you recall a time when you put limits on what Jesus can do by looking at a situation logically instead of "faith-fully"?

___

___

___

TouchPoint

Some translations record the amount as "two hundred denarii." One denarius is equivalent to one day's pay, which translates into the accumulated wages of 200 days' work—nearly eight months!

Philip factored the cost. But he didn't factor in Jesus. He overlooked the obvious answer—Jesus—by determining the problem insurmountable.

STEP INTO THE UPPER ROOM

The most intimate setting in all of literature is found in the Gospel accounts of the Upper Room on the eve of Jesus' arrest. It is positively brimming with raw emotion between Teacher and disciple, Master and servant… and Friend-to-friend. And it records another exchange between Jesus and Philip—revealing yet another touch.

Find a quiet space, my friend, to bask in the rich text of John 14:1-11. Linger long over these sacred words before moving forward.

What point was Jesus trying to impress upon them according to verse 7?

___

___

___

Jesus made a definitive statement—that by knowing Him, they would know the Father as well. That to see Him was to see God.

Look back at John 10:30 and fill in the missing personal pronoun and verb:

"____________ and the Father ____________ one."

There was a truth Jesus tried to make clear leading up to this grand finale. Though difficult to grasp, it is a truth Jesus tried to help them understand more than once.

According to John 14:8, what was Philip asking?

____

I don't doubt the sincerity of Philip's question. I think he really wanted to see God (who wouldn't?). And he obviously felt comfortable enough to ask; "Lord, show us." The others may have wondered, but Philip had to ask. And thankfully he did. If he had not, we wouldn't have the answer! We have this priceless jewel of a response from Jesus that helps to make several things clear.

How often have we demanded of God; "Show me"? And—instead of warranted lightning bolts—been met with grace?

I don't doubt many harsh critics have passed judgment upon Philip's request.

But not Jesus.

Jesus didn't mind repeating Himself—this was too important. Jesus did not mete out disparaging remarks. He took a nurturing stance to foster faith.

WHEN REALMS COLLIDE

John 14:11

Believe me when I say that I am in the Father and the Father is in me; or at least believe on the evidence of the works themselves.

Jesus was speaking of the spiritual, while Philip was stuck on the physical. So Jesus went there with him. Philip wanted to see the Father. And Jesus' response? To paraphrase verse 11; "If you can't believe I and the Father are one [what you can't see], believe the miracles [what you can see]."

Jesus employed Philip's personality—his tendency to be sensible and practical. What caused him to doubt and raise the question Jesus was all-to-patient to answer could be used to help instead of hinder.

Jesus told him; "Believe me" ... be convinced ... persuaded. If Philip really thought about all he had witnessed, he would reach the conclusion that he had, in fact, seen God. He just needed to be guided in that direction.

So I wonder, was his faith weak ... or was it possibly just his personality type that needed coaching?

How many "Philips" are there? The skeptical ... unsure ... logical folks who demand proof?

One was enough for Jesus to take time to explain such deep theology. Enough for Jesus to encourage all mankind; "Do not let your hearts be troubled. Trust in God; trust also in me." (John 14:1)

TouchPoint

Another apostle, Paul, recorded a prayer we can all use when understanding seems elusive: "I pray that the eyes of your heart may be enlightened in order that you may know the hope to which he has called you, the riches of his glorious inheritance in his holy people."

Ephesians 1:18

DAY 3

What's in a Personality

Oh the wonder of God's vast creation!

Don't you find yourself amazed at the sheer variety of species of… pick a category. Any category. Say, frogs. Or how about human personalities?

The study of temperaments began with Hippocrates (circa 460-370 B.C.) and was developed into more of a personality theory in the late 1700s by Immanuel Kant. Great advances were made in this area by Carl Jung in 1921 and then by Timothy Leary in the 1950s.

TouchPoint

It has been noted that Queen Esther may have been a ENTP while Mary, mother of Jesus, may have been classified as ISFJ.

InterVarsity Christian Fellowship/USA, 2013

The Myers-Briggs Type Indicator is a method used to determine someone's personality type. With this method, four distinct aspects of personalities have been identified. Each aspect reflects one of two possible orientations, resulting in a total of sixteen basic personality types:

Extrovert (E)	/	Introvert (I)
Sensing (S)	/	Intuition (N)
Thinking (T)	/	Feeling (F)
Judging (J)	/	Perceiving (P)

Knowing these traits gives us better insight into our own behavior and helps us to use them to their fullest advantage. Not only to see what best fits our personality type… but what doesn't. This understanding helps to guide our decisions on when to say yes… and when to say no.

You can actually participate in an online questionnaire to arrive at a more accurate result. What would you guess your type to be?

A PERSONALITY ALL HIS OWN

We can find four situations recorded in the Gospels where Philip is mentioned beyond those that merely list the apostles' names. In three of the four, Philip is asking questions. He was a man who wanted answers. Philip was a "facts and figures" kind of guy. We have seen how he was practical-minded, mathematical, and even somewhat cynical.

Discover what happened the day after Jesus fed the 5,000 by reading John 6:25-59.

The people wanted to eat more

____

Jesus told them that He was

____

Look at verse 53. Circle what Jesus told them they were to do:

eat manna from heaven
eat my flesh
drink my blood
drink living water

Now read verses 60-69. What kind of teaching was this?

- ☐ **Offensive**
- ☐ **Common**
- ☐ **Hard**
- ☐ **Easy**

Verse 66 tells us what resulted:

____

"I am the bread of life. Whoever comes to me will never go hungry, and whoever believes in me will never be thirsty."

(John 6:35)

Many of Jesus' teachings were difficult… radical. Even followers referred to as "disciples" turned away at some of His remarks. Philip may have asked a lot of questions, but he never fell away. Ultimately, he believed and obeyed his Lord's commands of the Gospel.

What else can we learn of Philip? In his book *12 Ordinary Men*, John MacArthur points out that he could also be viewed as pessimistic. He writes: "He was the type that would be more obsessed to find reasons why something can't be done rather than finding ways to do them."

Do you know someone with that disposition?

Jesus recognized his personality. As He did all of His disciples. And what a diverse group they were! There were no two alike. But Jesus showed them how to use their personalities to carry out His mission, to the glory of God.

So regardless of personality, they were used by God—proving all the more that God's power is indeed made perfect in weakness (2 Corinthians 12:9).

Has Jesus had to overcome something of your personality in order for you to believe what He has said about Himself?

Yes / No

If yes, explain: ______________________

____

____

____

Over at Personality Café, the supposition has been made that Philip's personality type was INTP (Introvert / Intuitive / Thinker / Perceiver). (Maher, 2013) Whatever it may be classified as, it was viewed as useful to Jesus.

It takes all kinds to build a church.

Beyond skills, abilities, and experience, we must include consideration of personality in ministry. It takes all kinds to build a church. Variety in personality is, after all, its success… not its downfall.

DAY 4

Camouflaged Usefulness

We played the tourist when family came for a visit and ventured into downtown Atlanta to tour Margaret Mitchell's home. A small museum has been added on to the house to display many of her personal effects—one of which is the typewriter she used to author her *Gone With the Wind* manuscript.

As I eyed the prized item, I asked my daughter if she knew what it was.

She had no clue.

None of the kids did.

What the adults could easily identify, the kids could not. We saw its usefulness. They could not.

We knew its purpose. They did not.

Can that translate with the way Jesus views people? He can see in them their potential... their usefulness. We don't always, do we?

Sometimes when I consider the diversity and the wide range of personalities of the twelve apostles, I catch myself wondering if I would have agreed with His selection.

How often is the obvious unseen to the untrained eye? Usefulness can, at times, be shrouded in camouflage—undiscovered even by the individual.

IT TAKES ALL KINDS

Imagine, for a moment, the type of team you would need to assemble to start a new business. What are some of the positions you would need to fill? What personalities would best fit those positions?

What about a church? What types of personalities are needed to head up the different ministries in a church?

Match a trait to a ministry:

Extrovert	**Children's**
Organized	**Planning**
Analytic	**Greeters**
Mathematical	**Youth**
Visionary	**Administrative**
Fun-Loving	**Education**
Scholarly	**Finance**

What about the apostles? Would you say they, too, had a variety of personalities?

IN ADDITION TO PERSONALITY

Now we all know about the unique talents and skills God has gifted to each of us to use to serve God's people in the name of Jesus. God can use our personalities to serve His purposes, as well. All our personalities can have faith. And to our faith are made additions.

Check all that apply according to 2 Peter 1:5:

- ☐ **Add to your faith, goodness**
- ☐ **Add to goodness, knowledge**
- ☐ **Add to knowledge, self-control**
- ☐ **Add to self-control, perseverance**
- ☐ **Add to perseverance, godliness**
- ☐ **Add to godliness, mutual affection**
- ☐ **Add to mutual affection, love**

Regardless of our personality, by God's power, goodness, and grace, we may all "participate in the divine nature." And the transforming touch of Jesus builds Christian character.

We are instructed to continue to grow in these Christ-like virtues—beyond our knowledge of Christ—in increasing measure. And when we do…

2 Peter 1:8 tells us it will prevent us from becoming

____________________ and ____________________

The New Living Translation reads: "The more you grow like this, the more productive and useful you will be in your knowledge of our Lord Jesus Christ."

No matter what our personalities may be, they can be used by God. How often have I thought; "I can't possibly be useful to God because I'm this. Or because I'm that?" When these questions arise (and they will) we must always return to the truth that we are useful only because of Jesus Christ.

What does 2 Corinthians 3:5 tell us about our competency?

By the grace of God we are used. And by the grace of God we are made useful.

"If you want to be of use to God, maintain the proper relationship with Jesus Christ by staying focused on Him, and He will make use of you every minute you live."
Oswald Chambers

Philip was perfectly suited for his calling—as were all the apostles.

Jesus, in His perfect wisdom, chose him as one of the Founders of the church. Jesus saw in him what no one else did—even now! He was greatly used in the spread of the gospel. Non-canonical records of early church history tell us that after Pentecost he preached in Greece, Syria, and Phrygia and that he was one of the first to suffer martyrdom.

This disciple, turned apostle, turned evangelist was more effective **after** receiving the Holy Spirit than before. *Shouldn't the same be said of us?*

When all was said and done—from the blunders in the Upper Room to final fruitfulness—Philip was used by God to further the kingdom of Christ, as were all the various personality types of the apostles.

Think about the different personality types of the servants of your home congregation. Do you see the different traits?

Do you notice how well that suits their involvement?

When we see the variety, we realize that each type would be missed if they weren't a part of the Body. Often we allow our differences to separate us when we need to celebrate our difference and see how they work together to accomplish a common goal ... the mission of sharing Jesus.

Complete 2 Corinthians 2:14:

But thanks be______________ ____________, who always leads us as captives in Christ's triumphal procession and________________ us to________________________ .

DAY 5

The Chosen

In our study of Philip this week we have seen how he reacted in only a couple of situations. While we can reach a few general conclusions about his personality type, we must refrain from becoming critical. We might have a tendency to focus on his human flaws, but it is imperative that we remember that **it was the Lord that chose him**.

I must honestly admit that I sometimes find myself being overly critical of different biblical personalities. Do you find yourself critical of any characters in the Bible? If so, who?

Do you ever catch yourself being critical of those God has placed in leadership roles within the church?

No doubt, there is much to be learned from the various people in the Bible. We can learn from their accomplishments and their failures. And should we find ourselves judging harshly, it would be prudent to remember that they were ordinary folks, chosen and used by God to perpetuate His promise and His plan.

Look at Luke 6:13-16 and complete Jesus' actions:

TouchPoint

apostolos—a Greek word meaning "one sent forth." An apostle was an agent commissioned to represent Jesus and was sent out by Him to be His messenger.

________________ **His disciples to Him**

________________ **twelve of them**

________________ **them apostles**

List some of the purposes for which Jesus appointed them according to additional details given in Matthew 10:1 and Mark 3:14-15:

1) ________________

2) ________________

3) ________________

4) ________________

According to John 15:16, who chose whom?

From this same verse, circle the reason Jesus appointed them:

To gain fame, riches, and honor
To promote peace
To bear eternal fruit

Jesus **called** His disciples to Him, **chose** the Twelve purposefully, and **appointed** them as apostles. He gave them authority to accomplish His set purposes and sent them out as His representatives. He did not do this arbitrarily.

Look at Luke 6:12-13. Check what Jesus did prior to selecting the apostles:

- ☐ **He went to a mountainside**
- ☐ **He conducted business as usual**
- ☐ **He spent the night in prayer**
- ☐ **He cast lots**

Jesus chose the apostles purposefully . . . and *prayerfully*. (As should anyone being selected for a position within the church.) He didn't say a quick prayer in passing for good measure. He didn't merely pause to ask God to bless what He had already decided to do. No! The text says that He prayed all night.

Jesus chose, appointed, instructed, and then empowered His apostles for a set purpose.

These Twelve, along with the later addition of Saul of Tarsus, were chosen specifically as apostles. But there are others chosen by God.

Matthew 10:2-4

"These are the names of the twelve apostles: first, Simon (who is called Peter) and his brother Andrew; James son of Zebedee, and his brother John; Philip and Bartholomew; Thomas and Matthew the tax collector; James son of Alphaeus, and Thaddaeus; Simon the Zealot and Judas Iscariot, who betrayed him."

LIVING AS CHOSEN

The apostle Peter penned a designation of who we are in Christ Jesus.

Complete 1 Peter 2:9:

"But____,

a royal priesthood, a holy nation, God's special possession,

that you may declare the praises of him who called you

out of darkness into his wonderful light."

Now, you might feel a bit uncomfortable at the thought of being "chosen" (and that is what you are!), but doesn't it make you feel blessed? Significant? Like your life has purpose?

What did the apostle Paul say we are as God's chosen people in Colossians 3:12? (Circle all that apply to you):

Sinful	**Holy**
Dearly Loved	**Loathed**

But with that comes an expectation. List what we are to wear:

- ______________________________
- ______________________________
- ______________________________
- ______________________________
- ______________________________

Inhabited by the Holy Spirit and clothed with these virtues we can live fruitful lives as the chosen people of God. And by these, there can be unity—even in our differences.

The glorious truth is that God is able to work through **each** of us, using our strengths and overshadowing our weaknesses, to accomplish our shared mission in Christ.

Rather than see negative traits in Philip, Jesus saw his usefulness to the Kingdom. Now it is ours to share that touch in a coming together of all our personalities to exclaim as Philip: "Come and see the Messiah."

WEEK FOUR
Matthew, the Changed

DAY 1
Called Out

Change.

You either love it. Or you hate it.

The thought of it can evoke panic, anxiety, or fear.

Or it might bring relief, excitement, or even joy.

I guess it depends on the starting point.

> **How do you typically respond to change?**
>
> **Can you name a recent incident of change? Its cause; your response; the outcome?**
>
> **Where in your life might you need change?**

TouchPoint

"The world does need changing, society needs changing, the nation needs changing, but we never will change it until we ourselves are changed."

Billy Graham, The Westminster Collection of Christian Quotations

SITTIN' ON READY

Let's see how the Lord's disciple, Matthew, handled change.

Little is said about Matthew in all of the New Testament. He kept very much to the background, which signifies a humility about him. He mentions himself only twice in his own Gospel (his call and his name among the list of all the disciples.)

It is obvious he knew and loved the Hebrew Scriptures. According to Paul Benware's *New Testament Survey*, he quoted from the Old Testament 53 times and made another whopping 76 allusions to them!

Read the calling of Matthew from the following accounts and note the differences:

Matthew 9:9:
Mark 2:14:

In his own Gospel, he refers to himself as Matthew—his Greek name, which means "gift of God." Mark and Luke use his Jewish name, Levi, when noting this same incident.

According to these same verses, what two actions does Matthew take in his response?

1. ______________________

2. ______________________

Matthew didn't hesitate in answering Jesus' call. He immediately followed Jesus.

First, he had to make a decision. And when he did, he chose to get up … act … obey.

He then had to make a commitment. And in that commitment, he followed.

To first follow, one must leave. There is something that is left behind when you choose to follow forward. Andrew and Peter left their nets. James and John left their father's business.

Is there something you must leave in order to follow your Lord more wholeheartedly?

Reflect upon the added detail provided in Luke 5:28:

"Levi got up, ______________ ____________________ and followed him."

For Matthew, his following was sacrificial. His tax booth, near *The Way of the Sea*, a busy commercial trade route in Capernaum, would have been lucrative. Unlike the fishermen, he would not be able to return to his tax collectors booth. For Matthew, there was no turning back.

But I believe Matthew was ready. Ready for change. Jesus called him. *Him*! Imagine! A man never chosen for anything. He was scorned and deemed an outcast culturally and religiously.

The religious leaders of the day condemned Matthew as a traitor. He would have been considered ritually "unclean" and forbidden to enter any synagogue. (*Isn't that equivalent to keeping sinners out of church?*)

Because tax collectors worked for Rome, he would have been loathed and rejected by his own countrymen. Often they were dishonest and corrupt, behaving like thugs. John MacArthur noted in *12 Ordinary Men* that they were "more worthy of scorn than the occupying Roman soldiers."

Look at Luke 5:32 in the sidebar and circle your selection:

Jesus called:

- **A) The beautiful**
- **B) The perfect**
- **C) The religious**
- **D) Sinners**

What did He call them to?

- **A) Try harder**
- **B) Repentance**
- **C) Self-Righteousness**
- **D) Give more**

Luke 5:32

"I have not come to call the righteous, but sinners to repentance."

Jesus calls sinners to repent, which means to change course. The first change that needs to occur is a change in direction. Following Jesus brings about change; but change begins with repentance. It is an inward change of heart back to God by following Jesus. Otherwise you might be following wrongly. Mark 3:7-8 is but one passage that shows people following Jesus for all the wrong reasons.

THE COST TO FOLLOW

We have already seen that it was financially sacrificial for Matthew to follow Jesus. Jesus would soon set the standard and clearly define the cost to follow Him.

Let's now listen to what the Master has to say about the high cost of discipleship.

Write Luke 14:33:

____

____

What are some costly choices you have had to make to follow Jesus?

List the three things Jesus teaches us that His disciples must do according to Mark 8:34.

1) ____

2) ____

3) ____

We see this touchableness in Matthew—a willing condition of heart to be touched by Jesus for good. He made a decision and acted upon it. He then made a commitment to be all-in. He didn't continue to collect taxes part-time and follow Jesus when it was convenient. And he left everything of his old life behind, trusting Jesus with his future. And, as we'll see tomorrow, he made his choice public knowledge.

Dear sister, Jesus calls us to follow Him. Know that He also brings about the change necessary that we may do so.

DAY 2

Cause for Celebration

I love reasons to celebrate. Oh, I don't just mean the biggies, like birthdays and such. Not just the milestone life-events but growing accomplishments, personal victories. I guess it's the practice of celebrating I like. Sharing joy. Just ask my kids. They'll tell you that I jump at any chance to stick a candle in a cupcake or run out for a celebratory ice cream cone.

And I especially love reasons to celebrate God: Jesus' birth ... His resurrection ... Sunday worship ... daily journal entries ... endless praise.

A HEART'S RESPONSE

Sometimes we get it right.

It is a modern-day custom to have a celebration following a major event. Like a reception after a wedding. But celebrating a significant experience is hardly anything new.

Moses and Miriam broke out into song upon their deliverance from Egyptian slavery through the waters of the Red Sea (Exodus 15). And when the psalmist remembered it in worship, he declared; "Come, let us rejoice in him" (Psalm 66:6).

When the long-misplaced ark was finally returned to the City of God, David celebrated before the Lord (2 Samuel 6:21).

As did Matthew.

Matthew experienced the ultimate touch of Jesus: the hope of change.

And his heart could hardly refrain from responding in joyous celebration.

In the midst of another harrowing day, Jesus showed up and selected him! He could put the past behind him and follow into a future now filled with hope.

Why, he was in the presence of Joy Himself. And when you're in the presence of Joy, you have joy! And he wanted everyone to know it!

Consider Matthew's response once he chose to get up, and leave everything behind, and committed to follow Jesus by reading Matthew 9:9-13.

Psalm 66:1-6

Shout for joy to God, all the earth! Sing the glory of his name; make his praise glorious. Say to God, "How awesome are your deeds! So great is your power that your enemies cringe before you. All the earth bows down to you; they sing praise to you, they sing the praises of your name. Come and see what God has done, his awesome deeds for mankind! He turned the sea into dry land, they passed through the waters on foot—come, let us rejoice in him."

What happened next?

Why do you have a banquet?

What did he have to celebrate?

What does it signify to have dinner with someone?

Matthew rushed home to celebrate and share a meal with his Friend. He didn't keep his decision private or compartmentalize this aspect of his life into something he kept separate. John MacArthur commented; "[Matthew] dropped everything immediately when he met Jesus, and in the joy of his newfound [life] and relationship, he embraced the outcasts of this world and introduced them to Jesus."

Who did the guest list include?

Why do you suppose all the undesirables attended Matthew's banquet?

Matthew wanted his friends to meet Jesus to celebrate his new calling… his new hope… his new life in Christ. He celebrated the old life left behind and the promised new life ahead.

Who do you know to invite to meet your Friend Jesus?

Matthew, along with the sinners of Capernaum, rejoiced at the grace and mercy shown this fellow outcast at the touch of Jesus.

TouchPoint

The Hebrew word quoted here for mercy is *hesed*, or steadfast love.

How might you celebrate His mercy and grace?

Write what it was that Jesus wanted the Pharisees to learn from Matthew 9:13:

____

The Pharisees could not believe that Jesus wanted to be associated with those who surrounded Him. They did not approve of the type of people He chose to be seen with in public.

Are there those with whom you don't want to be seen in public?

Jesus was quick to show them their error in attitude: their lack of mercy.

How do you define mercy?

Look up Hosea 6:6, the Old Testament remark Jesus is quoting.

Note what the following verses have to say about mercy:

Proverbs 28:13

____

Micah 6:8

____

THE MERCY OF OUR LORD

There were several observations I made in studying all three of the Gospel accounts regarding the calling of Matthew (Matthew 9:9-13; Mark 2:14-17; Luke 5:27-32). One of them was that all three record the banquet. But the most profound is the account it follows: the healing of the paralytic.

Matthew 9:6

"But I want you to know that the Son of Man has authority on earth to forgive sins." So he said to the paralyzed man, "I tell you, get up, take your mat and go home."

In this New Testament passage, four friends bring a paralyzed man to Jesus for healing. They go so far as to lower him through the roof! But the most telling part of the occasion is not the physical healing, but the authority Jesus demonstrated He has to forgive sin.

It was friends who sought healing from Jesus in this account. And now it is Matthew being the friend in bringing Jesus to his friends—sinners in need of spiritual healing.

Complete Luke 5:31:

Jesus answered them, "It is not the___________________

who need a_____________ , but the________________ .

I have not come to call the_________________________ ,

but_____________________________ to repentance."

I believe the "healthy" comment was directed at the Pharisees. You see, I don't think they felt they needed a physician for healing. I don't know about you, my friend, but I don't ever go to the doctor when I think I'm healthy—but only when I realize my need, because I willingly admit I'm sick.

And isn't our sin the soul-cancer that desperately needs healing?

It starts with recognizing our need for healing. Isn't that precisely what forgiveness is? Healing?

Jesus came to meet our greatest need ... that of a Savior.

We read that first the paralytic received spiritual healing by the forgiveness of his sin. And then of his physical healing at the hands of The Master Physician. We see Jesus mercifully surrounding Himself with sinners in need of forgiveness, as the proud stand aloof—untouched.

All the while Matthew, the forgiven, is found rejoicing over the grace and mercy extended the former-outcast.

Won't you join in the celebration?

DAY 3

Change, and More Change

It started with Jesus' first miracle in Cana when He changed water to wine.

He's been changing things ever since!

A GREATER CHANGE COMING

There was change in the religious order foretold throughout ancient Hebrew prophecies.

What would change according to the prophecy written in Jeremiah 31:31-32?

Read Ezekiel 21:26 and record what the Sovereign Lord says:

What do you see changing here?

The turban refers to the priesthood; and the crown, the kingship. Though Ezekiel shared the Lord's message of coming judgment upon the Israelites at the hands of Babylon, I believe it foreshadows the greater change coming.

The long-prophesied, long-awaited Messiah about whom Matthew wrote, that would take the eternal throne as King, was none other than Jesus Himself.

And the priesthood? That would change, too.

What could be said of the religious leaders of Matthew's day? They were Jewish, holy, elite, trained, law-abiding. Their position was inherited and revered.

I find it rather ironic that Matthew's Jewish name is Levi. Levi was one of the twelve sons of Jacob, as well as an original tribe of Israel. The priests, because of their lineage, were referred to as Levitical. And now this Levi would be one of the first in the new priesthood!

Common, ordinary, sinful Matthew—chosen first to follow as a disciple, then designated an apostle—would be one of the founding fathers of Christ's church, the new religious order of priests. Tax collectors and sinners, once expelled from the synagogue, were now the invited... welcomed into the House of God.

TouchPoint

What are some of the other changes ushered-in with the Lord's church?

"[Jesus] is the propitiation for our sins, and not for ours only but also for the sins of the whole world."

1 John 2:2 ESV

"Unlike the other high priests, he does not need to offer sacrifices day after day, first for his own sins, and then for the sins of the people. He sacrificed for their sins once for all when he offered himsel."

Hebrews 7:27

In the synagogue "people gathered for prayer and worship on the seventh day of the week."

Merrill C. Tenney, New Testament Survey, p. 82

Another change in the religion of God's people would be a move from external to internal.

Consider what kept the religious far from God according to Mark 7:6-8.

Continue reading Jeremiah 31:33-34.

Draw a line to complete the change according to God's promises:

He will write His law	**From the least**
Our sins	**Upon our hearts**
All would know the Lord	**Are forgiven**

THE PROBLEM OF SIN

At the dedication of the temple, Solomon uttered in his prayer; "There is no one who does not sin." (2 Chronicles 6:36) His father, David, wrote what God looks for when he looks down upon mankind.

What sticks out to you when reading Psalm 14:2-3?

From Isaiah 59:2, write down what it is that separates us from God.

The inerrant Word of God teaches us that Jesus is the Answer to our sin problem. He came to save us from our sins (Matthew 1:21) and to reconcile us back to God (Colossians 1:20-22), something the old sacrificial system could not do. Jesus taught that by His blood we receive forgiveness of sin (Matthew 26:28) and that there is a necessary rebirth (John 3:1-5)—that through the waters of baptism we are buried with and reborn in Christ and receive the essential Holy Spirit.

The Epistles elaborate more fully how it is by the grace of God—through faith—that we are saved (Ephesians 2:8). That there is not one that is righteous, for there is nothing we can do to earn our salvation.

Titus 3:5

"He saved us, not because of righteous things we had done, but because of his mercy. He saved us through the washing of rebirth and renewal by the Holy Spirit."

RIGHTING RIGHTEOUSNESS

Remember the remark Jesus made when the Pharisees confronted Him at Matthew's banquet? He stated that He had not come to call the righteous ... particularly the self-righteous!

Another change in the landscape of religiosity was the Source of righteousness, a dire problem in Jesus' day. Righteousness was then (and sometimes even still) viewed as a matter of keeping the law. We see evidence of this in the Gospels, but especially in Paul's letter to the Romans.

Soak in Romans 3:20-22 then complete the following:

According to Verse 20, who will be declared righteous in keeping the law?

Complete verse 21:

______________ ______________ ______________ from the law the righteousness of God has been made known, to which the Law and the Prophets testify.

What does "BUT NOW" say to you?

According to verse 22, righteousness is given through ______________________________________

Righteousness is not derived from self. It cannot be earned, secured by our performance, or achieved by observing the law (Galatians 3:11). Any and all righteousness we have is not our own, but Christ's alone (Philippians 3:9). The self-righteous, you see, do not see the need for Jesus' righteousness. (Much like the healthy not needing the doctor.)

THE AUTHORITY OF ONE

There would then, too, be a shift in authority from that of the High Priest and the teachings of the Law and the Prophets to the authority of Jesus Christ.

Ten times in Matthew's Gospel—a Gospel that contains more of Jesus' teachings and discourses than the others—he quoted a frequent comment Jesus made when preaching and teaching.

Matthew 28:18

"Then Jesus came to them and said, "All authority in heaven and on earth has been given to me."

There was a common phrase Jesus used when teaching of the kingdom of God and His Christ. Look up Matthew 5:22, and write the first four words quoted:

Jesus resolved man's sin problem. He changed the priesthood and religion. He expanded the kingdom of heaven culturally and geographically. And He changed the way we relate to and serve God and man.

Glory!! Now that's some change!

DAY 4

Relational Change

You can go to church your entire life and know religion. But it isn't until you meet Jesus that things change between you and God.

I was raised in a church steeped in tradition ... *religion*. Going to church was just something you did (or so it seemed to me).

It was architecturally beautiful, as it was decorated with the finest artwork and artifacts. But when I remember it, my mind instantly goes to the cold, hard marble and the echo of litanies' chant.

It wasn't until many years later that I learned the difference between attending church and worship. That it was personal ... *relational*. That it was about meeting and befriending Jesus, ***my*** Savior and Redeemer.

All those changes Jesus made to religion that we looked at yesterday? They removed the barriers that kept people from God. And God Incarnate—Jesus, the God Who Came Near—provided the way to enter into relationship with our Heavenly Father.

Record God's response from John 14:23:

____

FAMILY MATTERS

Jesus changed the method and means of relating to God from one of religion to relationship.

Write the number of the corresponding Bible verse next to its truth.

Christianity is, foremost, fellowship with God through Christ.

_____ **The Way to the Father**	**1) 1 John 1:3**
_____ **Mutual knowledge**	**2) Romans 8:16**
_____ **We enjoy fellowship**	**3) John 10:14**
_____ **God's promise as Father**	**4) John 14:6**
_____ **We are made children**	**5) 2 Corinthians 6:18**
_____ **Testimony of the Spirit**	**6) Galatians 3:26**

Jesus brought change to mankind's relationship with their Creator. But integrating all these changes within the heart of man and in fellowship with the Trinity and fellow-man would require Him to leave those He came to save.

Romans 8:9

"You, however, are not in the realm of the flesh but are in the realm of the Spirit, if indeed the Spirit of God lives in you. And if anyone does not have the Spirit of Christ, they do not belong to Christ."

John 16:7 explains why Jesus' leaving was crucial. What would happen?

THE SPIRIT CHANGES EVERYTHING

The apostle Paul had much to say about the essential work of the Holy Spirit, not only in each believer but in the church, as well.

Open your Bible to Ephesians and read 2:11-22. Answer the following questions.

What was the dilemma?

____

____

____

What was the solution?

____

____

____

The Gentiles were once separate, excluded, and strangers to the "covenants of the promise, without hope and without God." And then we read that blessed phrase once again; "But now" (verse 13)! In Christ they are now brought near and included in the family of God.

Complete the following portion of verse 14:

"Who has made the _______________ _________ and has _______________ the ____________________, the dividing wall of _______________"

What is the purpose stated in verse 15?

____

Complete how is this accomplished:

Through ___________________, by the _______________

Who are we now (verses 19-21)?

__________________________________ **citizens**

Members of ____________________________________

A holy ____

God now resides in this dwelling by

____ .

In Christ, we are united to God and one another through the Holy Spirit. Though we are now many, there is unity into one body by the Spirit.

As Jesus brought change to religion and all Persons of the Trinity to relationship with God and man, tomorrow we'll see that the Spirit is the One that is the Power behind our personal transformation.

DAY 5

Transformational

It was 1994.

She wasn't entirely sure what she'd agreed to do, but she was more ready than she knew.

She climbed the mounting stairs, second-guessing her yes only to be met with a warmth so rare.

The streaming light captivated her. The contrast only served to accentuate the deep, dark void in her heart... her life. A life lacking joy... Hope. As the new life of a baby swelled within her, hope of her new life swelled, as well.

That long-lost woman that once dwelled in this old tent is now buried with Christ. And this new woman? She hasn't been the same ever since!

THE GIST OF CHANGE

A great example of transformation is the human life cycle. Human life transforms from egg, to infant, aging to adulthood, to death, and to life eternal, through many stages of drastic change all along the way.

There are other examples of transformation in nature: weather cycles, frogs, butterflies, and plants, to name a few.

Consider the seed. It dies; it germinates; it rises; it buds with new life in its veins; it grows; it expands; it multiplies; *it blesses.*

And we find it in the Bible, too. Just look at the seed of Abraham that has transformed into the kingdom of Christ.

Circle what Jesus is comparing this transformation to, according to Matthew 13:31-32?

Mustard plant
Vineyard
Kingdom of Heaven

Consider if it might also symbolize:

Jesus
The church
The individual believer
All 3

Match the change to its verse:

Crucified with Christ	**2 Corinthians 5:17**
To live a new life	**Colossians 3:10**
The old is gone	**Galatians 2:20**
Made new in attitude	**Romans 6:4**
Renewed to image of Creator	**Ephesians 4:23**

The people Jesus miraculously healed were changed physically… externally (like the lepers, for instance). But His disciples He changed from the inside out. He changed their hearts. And their character followed. But isn't that change also visible? Can't it, too, be seen in one's lifestyle and actions?

Note the differences of those that live by the flesh and those who live led by the Spirit from Galatians 5:19-26.

____

____

____

Note the attitudes:

Acts 9:1______________________________________

Philippians 3:8__________________________________

TouchPoint

Acts 9:1 is Saul. Philippians 3:8 is Paul. Both are the same man. (*Or are they?*)

Write 2 Corinthians 3:18:

We are being transformed by the Spirit, into the likeness of Jesus, as an ongoing, lifelong process. Thanks be to God!

TRANFORMING TOUCH

Through our study of Matthew, we witnessed the all-encompassing plan that brought about significant change. We saw how God changed religion—from exclusive. How He changed the priesthood—from elite. And how he changed man's relationship with Him—from distant.

TouchPoint

Matthew lived out 2 Corinthians 5:17 not just 3-dimensionally, but in 4D!

And Matthew?

Matthew lived a changed life. He lived a redeemed life. A life of transformation—the life graced every Christian.

All this change we have seen at the hand of Jesus this week is not merely a touch. Jesus grabbed hold of Matthew, redeemed and reformed him and set him free—just as He changes every sinner to saint.

Perhaps you have experienced the transforming touch of Jesus in your life in some way. Maybe He has touched your heart, your mind, your relationships and brought about change.

Maybe He has changed your darkness ... to light. Your brokenness ... to new life. Your despair ... to dreams.

Are there areas that still need His healing touch?

Continue to follow close and hard after Him. He is able to renew all things (and He is patient in the process).

In the form of a rhetorical question, Genesis 18:14 confirms the hard truth of this and all matters—there is nothing too hard for the Lord! By the power of His Holy Spirit, we are changed in ever-increasing measure until that grand and glorious Day when we will all be changed ... for good.

WEEK FIVE

Jairus, the Desperate Parent

DAY 1

Parenting Pleas

My sweet son was only five. I had taken this pitifully sick child to the doctor thinking he had some common childhood ailment. I expected to waltz in, get a round of prescribed antibiotics, and return home that same day to nurse him back to good health. When doctor after doctor from the practice came in to examine him, my level of concern piqued. The crescendo came when the doctor explained that my son would need to be transported to a children's hospital for further testing. She proceeded to share her medical opinion and all that entailed.

My first response? Prayer.

My first thought? Jesus. And His name played on repeat, over and over in my mind. When she left the room, I made my first phone call—right to the church, to request the prayers of the elders.

A FATHER'S PETITION

The desperation of a concerned parent over a suffering child is about as predictable as a blazing wildfire. It can be driven by several factors—hopelessness, fear, chronic stress—but the underlying generator is, undeniably, love.

Let me introduce you to this week's profile by reading all three Gospel accounts in Matthew 9:18-19; Mark 5:21-24; and Luke 8:40-42.

TouchPoint

Synagogue rulers could be viewed as a servant of God. They were viewed as a sort of governor of the synagogue. They served as caretakers and worship leaders. Most were also Pharisees and teachers.

What is the father's name?

What is his profession?

What can you learn of his daughter?

What bodily position did he take from Matthew 9:18?

How is it described in Mark 5:22?

Of what does this position remind you?

Have you ever fallen on your knees before Jesus in prayer for a child?
Describe:

____

____

____

In humility and respect, this religious leader came to Jesus, earnestly pleading that He heal his dying daughter. He knelt at His feet—reminiscent of prayer—making a petition on her behalf.

And he came in faith.

We don't know how much faith. But we do know that there was no precedent at this point of Jesus raising the dead.

But he believed.

He believed Jesus could heal *from the point of death.*

Circle the tense, according to Matthew 9:18:

Will die

Might die

Has died

Complete Jairus' statement of faith from Matthew 9:18:

"But come and put your hand on her, and
______________ ______________ ______________."

Read Matthew 9:23-24; Mark 5:37-40; and Luke 8:51-53 and describe the scene:

____

____

____

The fact that there were mourners already on the scene is proof that Jairus' daughter had already died. The description of the "commotion and wailing" is a depiction of inconsolable grief. There is no more dreadful noise than that of hopeless mourning. And there is no sorrow more deep than that over those who die without the hope of heaven.

TouchPoint

It was customary, especially for the more affluent leaders in a village, to hire professional mourners at the passing of a loved one.

But what is our faith, based on the truth of God's promise in Christ, according to 1 Thessalonians 4:14?

A SAVIOR'S RESPONSE

Now let's read the rest of the story. Let's not leave it with scoffers mocking Jesus. Let's not lock ourselves in the dark room of death but see the hope available, now that Jesus has come. After Jesus responds to this father's plea. After Jesus touches this daughter. Because the story doesn't end at her death.

Read the conclusion of the matter from Matthew 9:25-26; Mark 5:41-43; and Luke 8:54-55.

What stands out most to you?

I love Jairus' parenting approach. At the first sign of trouble he knows where to turn. He knows where his help comes from. But do you know what I love even more?

Psalm 121:2

"My help comes from the Lord, the Maker of heaven and earth."

Jesus' response.

From it we glean strength, hope, and encouragement. From it we see the heart of a Savior toward the despairing parent.

DAY 2

Where Stories Merge

When the three Gospel writers, under the divine direction of the Holy Spirit, recount the healing of Jairus' daughter, they tell of the occurrence of two miracles on the same occasion.

I also think that the other healing along the way to Jairus' home is no coincidence, for Jesus weaves the two together to teach a valuable lesson on faith.

A STUDY IN COMPARISONS

Let's read the masterful retelling by Luke to render their commonality.

Leviticus 15:19

"When a woman has her regular flow of blood, the impurity of her monthly period will last seven days, and anyone who touches her will be unclean till evening."

Read Luke 8:40-55.

The daughter was____________ years old (verse 42).

The woman was sick for_______ years (verse 43).

Jairus________ to Jesus (verse 41).

The woman ________________ to Jesus (verse 44).

There is the healing of Jairus'________ and the woman is called____________ by Jesus (verse 48).

Leviticus 21:11

"He must not enter a place where there is a dead body. He must not make himself unclean, even for his father or mother."

According to two laws in Leviticus (in the sidebar) touching both "daughters" will make

Jesus____ .

Where stories intersect and merge is the place of greatest gleaning.

Because of the similarities in these two stories, a deeper theme is revealed. What may appear at first glance to be an interruption to the task at hand actually causes one to ponder the providence of their meeting.

THE COMMON DENOMINATOR

Jairus and the woman both came to Jesus, bowing in desperation, faith and humility.

Now remember, Jairus is the ruler of a synagogue. He would be well-trained in all the elements of the Law. But the Law did not trump love. Because Jesus was touched by the woman, He would have been considered "unclean." And yet the man still allowed Jesus into his home—even to touch his daughter.

And Jesus would have been declared unclean yet again by touching the dead child. But that consideration did not hinder His compassion. He considered the need of the person over the letter of the Law.

The woman touched just the fringe of His garment and received enough power to be healed completely and instantly. Might Jairus have wondered if Jesus still had power enough to raise the dead?

Another touch of Jesus is the one of reassurance.

According to Luke 8:48, circle what the woman had:

Patience
Knowledge
Faith
Concern

According to Luke 8:50, circle what the father needed:

Fear
Faith
Money
Love

Jesus told the woman;

"Your _______________ has made you well" (verse 48).

Jesus told Jairus; "Do not fear, have________ " (verse 50).

What overcomes fear?____________________

The most common denominator with regard to Jesus' touch in both accounts was that of faith. Their faith was another worthy consideration over the Law.

The woman's faith was such that she believed if she but touched the edge of Jesus' cloak she would be healed. Jairus believed. But there was something to be learned from the woman's faith.

And might that precisely be a possibility why their paths crossed en route to Jairus' daughter?

Here—for the first time—Jesus tells us what overcomes fear. Faith!

TouchPoint

Pistis = faith, belief, trust. "Faith is always a gift from God, and never something that can be produced by people. In short, *pistis* (faith) for the believer is 'God's divine persuasion'—and therefore distinct from human belief."

Strong's Concordance

And Jesus teaches one crucial thing about faith, laying the fundamental foundation on which all New Testament writers will later expound.

Complete the blanks from Luke 8:48:

"Your____________________ has______________ you."

Read Ephesians 2:8 and note God's gift of grace that comes by faith:

____

The same faith that evoked the Lord's grace of healing for the woman and raised the dead daughter is the same faith that—by God's grace—saves.

Jesus does not back away from the unclean. But draws near those that approach Him in faith—with grace to save.

DAY 3

Prayers of a Parent

Let's continue along with Jairus, as he makes his way to the answer of his request to Jesus. For the journey he makes with Jesus doesn't just span the distance to his destination, but also to what is lacking in his knowledge of faith. And it is a teaching journey for us, as well.

We gazed upon the faith lesson he learned from the woman. Jesus told the woman—within Jairus' hearing—"Your faith has healed you." And later Jesus told him to "believe" and his daughter, too, would be healed. That he need not fear, but entrust her unto Him.

When it comes to the well-being of the child, Jesus made one request... for faith.

And today we come to the second lesson to be gained from Jairus' encounter with Jesus. That of a parent. Specifically, a praying parent.

I firmly believe Jairus models a praying parent for us.

So let's travel there today. Let's look at Jesus' touch upon Jairus in answer to his petition and learn what application we can make as concerned parents or even grandparents.

TouchPoint

"When our hearts are full of God, sending up holy desires to the throne of grace, we are then in our highest state, we are upon the utmost heights of human greatness; we are not before kings and princes, but in the presence and audience of the Lord of all the world, and can be no higher, till death is swallowed up in glory."

William Law, Serious Call to a Devout and Holy Life

A GOOD WORD ON PRAYER

Jairus came to Jesus requesting healing for a loved one. Sound familiar? We have a word for that.

We call it________________________ .

It doesn't matter the age of the child—once a parent, always a parent. There are 90+ year-old parents residing at the senior living community where I am blessed to work who still stew about their children (no matter that they too are retired seniors). The majority of all parents, at some point, carry concern for their children. And there is no better place to carry that concern than to God's throne of grace.

The greatest act in *all* of parenting is that of prayer.

Prayer releases fear and frees us to parent with confidence and faith. Trusting our children into Father God's perfect heart and sovereign hands.

Praying is to move our parenting into the presence of God where we can parent in the attitude of faith. An attitude defined for us in 2 Timothy 1:7.

According to 2 Timothy 1:7, what are three "spirits" we embody?

1) ______________________________

2) ______________________________

3) ______________________________

Jairus approached Jesus to save his child's life. As do we—we pray to Jesus for the salvation that only comes through Him.

We need to pray for our child's salvation—even after baptism. We should include prayers for them to develop a deepening love for Jesus, His Word, and His church. We want for them what we ask for ourselves in our own prayers—to increasingly grow in faith and grace.

The greatest act in all of parenting is that of prayer.

Our prayers are a reflection of our hearts. As is our parenting. Jairus had love for his child and a desire to save her. And I'm just sure that is your heart for your child, as well.

The heart of a godly parent is the heart of a young couple I know through our church. When they were expecting their first child they were informed that once their baby was delivered she would not be able to survive outside the womb. The heart of that father was seen in his parenting—even of his unborn child. He had a desire that his daughter hear God's Word and know of her Heavenly Father's love. So they bought a children's story Bible and read it to her. Baby Faith heard God's Word from her parents own voice and loving hearts.

THE BIBLE ON PRAYER

The most powerful tool we have as a parent is the Bible. And not only for wisdom and discipleship. The Bible, among other things, is a book both *of* prayer and *on* prayer.

Match the prayers modeled for us with the Bible verse:

Judges 13:8	**Instruction regarding Jerusalem's suffering children**
2 Sam 12:16-17	**Man begs Jesus to help his only son**
2 Sam 12:22	**Parent's faith not to fear the king's edict**
Lam 2:18-19	**Pray as long as the child is alive**
Luke 9:38-42	**Royal official begs for his son's healing**
John 4:43-50	**King prays for his dying baby**
Heb 11:23	**Prayer for God to teach how to raise a son**

Let's delve into a response of Jesus to yet another request. A request for Him to teach on prayer. We'll close out today by looking at a few critical points Jesus made about prayer from Luke, Chapter 11.

Read Luke 11:1-13.

What is Jesus teaching in verses 5-8?

What three things does Jesus tell us to do?

A_______ _______

S_______ _______ _______

K_______ _______ _______ _______

How does Jesus compare God's response to that of an earthly father (verse 11-12)?

What is the greatest gift of all given in answer to prayer from verse 13?

Luke 11:9

"So I say to you: Ask and it will be given to you; seek and you will find; knock and the door will be opened to you."

Matthew 7:11

"If you, then, though you are evil, know how to give good gifts to your children, how much more will your Father in heaven give good gifts to those who ask him!"

TouchPoint

There are many great resources in conjunction with the Bible that are available to the praying parent. Two books to consider are:

Praying the Scriptures for Your Children

by Jodie Berndt

and

The Power of a Praying Parent
by Stormie Omartian

Jesus responds to the request of this disciple in multiple ways. He first teaches what and how to pray (vs 2-4), and He teaches to have boldness in asking (vs 5-8). He then encourages us to partner with God. We are taught the doing of prayer—our part in the asking, seeking, and knocking. He then shows us that God will do His part as any Father would. And then Jesus tells us of the gracious gift of the Holy Spirit—the Wisdom, Comfort, and Power to endure the cause of our asking.

Is there a prayer you prayed that you can now pause to give God praise and thanks for?

Is there a prayer you need now pray?

DAY 4

The "Faith-full-ness" of Prayer

You can't merely open the door on prayer and rush right past it. Prayer is much too grand to skip on by.

As "they" say, after all; "When opportunity strikes ... " So, since we're on the subject, what do you say we linger awhile?

This week we have seen Jairus come to Jesus with a request and we have seen Jesus respond, in asking for faith. How critical at this point then to merge the two inseparable components together—faith and prayer.

You can hardly have one without the other!

BEING "FAITH-FULL" IN PRAYER

Even now I pray for depth of insight; that your prayer life might strengthen faith and that faith might fill your every prayer.

In Luke 18 we read a parable of the persistent widow that Jesus told to illustrate an attitude of prayer. Jesus told His disciples; "Pray and do not lose heart." (Luke 18:1 ESV). How, in this crushing world, do we not "lose heart"?

We pray in faith.

Read James 5:13-16.

Verse 15 defines what is to be offered?

With what?

Jesus responds to faith. He speaks of the necessity of faith in both healing accounts we have been studying (Luke 8:48, 50).

Therefore, our prayers need the essential ingredient of faith.

Hebrews 11:6

"And without faith it is impossible to please God, because anyone who comes to him must believe that he exists and that he rewards those who earnestly seek him."

If you sometimes feel you have a lack of faith, don't be ashamed. Honestly confess that and ask for more—believing.

For faith to grow, we need the Word.

Circle the purpose of John's Gospel stated in John 20:31:

A) That you may believe
B) That you may be entertained
C) That you may be have life
D) That you may be left wondering

God's Word waters faith that it might grow. So if God's Word is needed for faith and faith is needed for prayer, it stands to reason that God's Word is valuable in prayer.

PRAYER'S ARSENAL

TouchPoint

"Little of the Word with little prayer is death to the spiritual life. Much of the Word with little prayer gives a sickly life. Much prayer with little of the Word gives more life, but without steadfastness. A full measure of the Word and prayer each day gives a healthy and powerful life."

Andrew Murray, Prayer Power

The most powerful weapon we have in prayer is the Bible.

Come, let's reason together...

Circle the completion of the following statement from 1 John 5:14:

"This is the confidence we have in approaching God: that if we ask anything______________________________, he hears us."

A) ...according to our wants ...
B) ...according to God's grace ...
C) ...according to God's will ...
D) ...according to my will ...

We can pray in confidence when we pray God's will. So where do we go to know His will?

Find the answer in John 15:7 and fill in the void:

"If you remain in me and______________________

__________________ remain in you, ask whatever you wish, and it will be done for you."

We are to pray in faith, according to God's will … and both come by the Word.

Faith comes from hearing God's Word and believing. Knowing God's will, too, is learned from His Word.

The Word is the apex of the triangle between faith and knowledge of God's will. Both are vital components of prayer.

It only goes to show, then, that praying His Word is to pray faith-fully, according to His will.

When we pray God's Word we can pray in faith, knowing we are praying:

His will

His truth

His promises;

and are releasing His Power

Each verse you memorize is another weapon to add to your prayer arsenal. A weapon to help demolish doubt, strangle strongholds, proclaim promise, or perpetuate peace.

Start watering your faith with these sacred words:

Read each verse listed below and note something to be applied to prayer.

Psalm 34:17

Isaiah 55:10-11

Jeremiah 1:12

John 16:23

James 5:16

Is there something for which you need to stop and pray—in faith and the Word—right now?

I say to you, as Jesus said to Jairus; "Do not be afraid, just believe."

DAY 5

Your Own Personal Touch

In this study we have been learning to recognize the touch of Jesus upon those in the Gospel record. By doing so, we can determine if we can identify with them (for it is from experience we best minister). That awareness prepares us to share that same sort of touch with someone in a similar circumstance.

Here, with Jairus, we have seen his petition to Jesus for healing and Jesus response. We have seen his need and Jesus' meeting that need.

We can now ask ourselves if we have shared that same experience. We may or may not be able to identify with him as a parent wanting desperately for a child to be saved. But we can identify with him in the area of praying in faith for a loved one.

So now it is ours to see if there are those among us whom we can encourage in their faith as they earnestly pray for another.

And there is something we can do in the area of prayer. We can add our own personal touch.

What is the compassionate touch of prayer on behalf of another?

THE INTERCESSORY TOUCH

Intercession—there is no more honored position than to bow before God on behalf of others.

And there is no more vital work we can do or more powerful and effective way to serve than to pray for the needs of others.

Paul issued two strong exhortations for us to heed regarding intercession.

TouchPoint

Intercessor: "One who goes between; a mediator; one who pleads on behalf of another."

Webster's Revised Unabridged Dictionary

Note his instruction from 1 Timothy 2:1:

Complete phrases from Ephesians 6:18:

. . . in the ____________________________

. . . on all ____________________________

. . . with all __________________________

. . . ________________________ keep on praying

. . . for ____________________ the Lord's people

What does it mean to intercede? Before we study examples in Scripture, we'll first look at the perfect depiction from Psalm 106:23.

Write Psalm 106:23 below:

____

____

____

There's a term in there we don't use often: "stand in the breach." The Hebrew word *bapperes* is used only twice in the Old Testament. Another translation is "to stand in the gap." (*Bible Hub/Englishman's Concordance*) That's just what intercession is. It's standing in the gap between an earthly need and Heaven's mercy seat. Just like Moses appealed to God on behalf of the Israelites, referenced in this verse.

PETITIONS ASKED . . . PETITIONS ANSWERED

There is no shortage of excellent examples in Scripture, which should give us clarity as to the importance of just such a practice for God's people.

Let's look at several.

Verse	Intercessor	For Whom	Outcome
Gen 18:20-23			
Exod 32:7-14			
Num 14:10-20			
Est 8:3-7; 9:1			
John 11:1-3; 43-44			
Rom 8:34			
Heb 7:25			

Just as Jesus intercedes for us, we are expected to intercede for others. That is no small task, my friend!

And it can be rather overwhelming at times in the face of such tragic adversity and suffering.

Scripture has a good word for us in that situation as well. Keep these handy as encouragement when it comes to this honorable duty…
and pray on.

According to Romans 8:26-27, Who is it that helps us?

Circle all the ways He helps:

In our weakness

When we don't know what to pray

When words escape us

When we are unsure of God's will

Complete Galatians 6:9:

"Let us___________ _____________ _________________

in doing good, for at the proper time we will reap a

harvest if_____ _________ _______ _____ _______ ."

Who can you stop to pray for right now?

"Now to him who is able to do immeasurably more than all we ask or imagine, according to his power that is at work within us, to him be glory in the church and in Christ Jesus throughout all generations, for ever and ever! Amen" (Ephesians 3:20-21).

WEEK SIX

A Greek Woman, the Different

DAY 1

Driving Faith

You always go where faith drives you.

She boldly stood before a room full of foreign men. But therein lay her only Hope.

It didn't matter to her that she was a Gentile. It didn't matter to her that she was a woman.

It didn't matter that she was different... *unwelcome.*

No, none of that mattered.

Because you always go where faith drives you.

And so it was that day for a Syrophoenician Woman.

NATIONALITY OF INCONSEQUENCE

TouchPoint

This "faith-full" woman is described differently in the Gospels. In Matthew's Gospel she is referred to as the Canaanite woman. In Mark's Gospel she is known as the Greek woman from Syrian Phoenicia. This is due largely in part to their differing audiences. But to Jesus it didn't matter. All He saw was her driving faith.

Jesus and His disciples had traveled from Capernaum to the Gentile city of Tyre, in Phoenicia (about 30 miles away). After feeding the multitudes, Jesus was looking for a quiet spot to teach them privately. That's where we find them huddled, when a Greek woman enters the scene.

Going all the way back to the book of beginnings—Genesis—who else is mentioned with the Canaanites in Genesis 9:25-26?

____

How did Isaac feel about them, according to Genesis 28:8

____

What did God promise regarding the Canaanites in Exodus 33:2

____

There was quite a history between the Canaanites and God's chosen people. Although there had long since been a land of Canaan, the woman of our study this week was still called a Canaanite. Use of this title likely would have conjured up instant innuendos among the Jewish people.

Read Matthew 15:21-28.

How did the woman refer to Jesus?

____

What does this acknowledge?

____

Mark 12:35

"While Jesus was teaching in the temple courts, he asked, 'Why do the teachers of the law say that the Messiah is the son of David?'"

She attested to her belief of His Messianic status. Use of the title "Son of David" makes reference to the royal bloodline of King David and associates Jesus with the long-promised Messiah of God.

What was her request?

____

How did the disciples respond?

____

____

Did that stop her? ________________________________

IDENTIFYING THE DIFFERENT
… In Yourself … In Others

As was the case with this woman in her day, there are people who come to our churches making a request of the Lord out of extreme need; but because they may be viewed as different, they are dismissed … or worse, rejected altogether. Unfortunately, there are occasions when we grievously err in deeming that someone doesn't fit in or belong or when we evaluate their need as bothersome or unworthy.

Have you witnessed such an occasion? If so, explain:

Jesus never denied the different. He is the Creator, Lover, and Sustainer of all things different. Why, He even became different.

In what ways would you be classified as different?

Tomorrow we will look more at Jesus' response. But for today, let's gaze upon the disciples' response and meditate upon the condition of our own hearts when it comes to the different.

The disciples seemed almost annoyed with her presence and her request. Her needs were overlooked for her differences. And she was overlooked due to the preoccupation with the task at hand.

Been there?

Done that?

Scripture records another time they were bothered by someone who didn't fit into their clique.

Read Matthew 19:13-15 and record your observations:

It is often all-too-easy to look upon the faults of the disciples and ignore one's own flaws. I can honestly (albeit, shamefully) admit that I am guilty of the same offense.

1 John 4:19

"We love because he first loved us."

Spend these closing minutes before God in prayer. Ask Him to open your eyes to see your attitude toward the different. Seek forgiveness, if necessary, of times when you have sleighted another because of it. Commit to change. And ask Him for grace to have the heart of Jesus toward others.

DAY 2

The Response of a Savior

The days of demon possessions were hard, indeed. And it was no exception for this mother. Her little girl suffered … and so did she.

She heard this man, this Son of David, was trying to hide out in a nearby home. She'd heard reports of the miracles He'd performed. So that's precisely where her faith carried her.

She entered His secret hiding place and threw herself to the ground before Him, pleading mercy. His followers urged that Jesus have her removed. But then Jesus made a rather curious reply.

Let's unwrap it together.

A PEOPLE'S PURPOSE

Read Matthew 15:21-28.

Select His first response noted in verse 23:

He invited her in
He acknowledged her pain
He gave no answer
He sent her away

Write what Jesus replied from verse 24:

____

____

Matthew 15:23-24

"Jesus did not answer a word. So his disciples came to him and urged him, 'Send her away, for she keeps crying out after us.'

He answered, 'I was sent only to the lost sheep of Israel.'"

Jesus, born a Jew into the house of Israel, went first and revealed Himself to the Jews. The salvation He offers was according to the promise of God for all mankind. So, why make this statement?

Now let's consider these passages in determining why Jesus may have made that comment. Match the letter to the Scripture:

______	**Deut 14:2**	**A) Source of salvation**
______	**John 4:22**	**B) They were a chosen people**
______	**Acts 13:46**	**C) Offered to the Jews first**
______	**Rom 1:16**	**D) Paul's practice in preaching**

The Hebrew people, later to become the Jewish nation of Israel, were chosen by God to perpetuate a promise resulting from man's sin problem. They were the first to be given God's promises, God's Covenants, His Law and commands, prophecies, and revealed Word. So, why not the gospel?

Read Matthew 10:5-6.

Where were the apostles first sent by Jesus?

____

THE CRUX OF THE MATTER

God chose a people to inherit a covenant of promise that would bless the entire world. Is there perhaps a distinguishing trait to be discerned as to why they were set apart?

TouchPoint

"The good news that Christ died for our sins, and that He rose from the dead to open eternal life, and that salvation is by grace through faith—all that is for everyone who believes. Not just Jews and not just Gentiles and no one race or social class or culture, but everyone who believes."

John Piper

What does Deuteronomy 9:6 tell us of their righteousness?

How are they described in Deuteronomy 31:27?

According to Deuteronomy 7:7-8, why did God redeem them from Egypt?

Man will be man—and so it was with Israel.

He chose a people for a particular purpose—not because they were better or more worthy. And I dare say it would not have gone any differently with any other people. Any nation He would have chosen would have become problematic—no matter their ethnicity.

Hebrews 11:1-2 notes what they *were* commended for: ________________________________

As we have seen in our study this far, Jesus commends faith. Jesus honored this woman's evident faith... above her nationality.

Jesus tested her, and her tenacity prevailed. And I believe He was teaching the apostles an important lesson at the same time. Different had become "us versus them."

Go back to Matthew 15:28. What was His final answer?

Ultimately, what is it that saves?

2 Corinthians 1:20a

"For no matter how many promises God has made, they are 'Yes' in Christ."

Jesus said "Yes." And God's final answer, through Christ, to His every promise to us is also a resounding "Yes!"

DAY 3

More On Different

Some words have a negative connotation. Like *stinky, morbid,* or *gruesome.*

And some words have a positive connotation. Like *yes, victory, all.*

Not "different." It's neutral. It's just... well, different.

But somewhere along the way, different became exclusionary. Different became an us versus them context.

And so it was between Gentile and Jew.

Genesis 18:18

"Abraham will surely become a great and powerful nation, and all nations on earth will be blessed through him."

From Genesis 18:18 in the sidebar, who would receive God's blessing through Abraham?

____

From the ancient days of Abraham, the promise of reconciliation to God and redemption from the curse of sin was for all people of every nation.

Check out the good news for us in Romans 1:16. The gospel brings salvation to

____.

And yet, when our Greek woman came calling upon Jesus, she was dismissed as different by the disciples.

IT TAKES TIME

What may have been some contributing factors to this change in attitude toward the Gentiles?

Draw a line connecting a verse with possible reasons for a growing divide among the camps:

Lev 20:23	**Viewed as the enemy**
Lev 20:26	**Customs angered God**
Num 33:55	**Determined unclean**
Deut 33:27	**Set apart from them**
Judges 6:9	**Seen as a snare**
Jer 30:22	**Often oppressed by them**
Acts 10:28	**God was their God alone**

It would seem that over the course of time the things the people of God knew to be true became distorted and altered. The intentions of God's heart were replaced by misinterpretations and traditions of men.

But there were those rare exceptions along the way.

EXCEPTIONAL EXCEPTIONS

Let's briefly look at two exceptions made with regard to outsiders and see what they represent.

Read Joshua 2:1; 8-13; 6:22-25.

Who helped the Israelite spies?

Where was she from?

What did she have, according to Hebrews 11:31?

Rahab was not excluded because of nationality, gender or profession. She is one of three Gentile women in Jesus' lineage. And she became part of the family of God because of her faith.

Read 2 Samuel 9:3-11.

Who received the king's blessing?

Complete 2 Samuel 21:7:

. . . because of the____________ between David and Jonathan.

What was done for Mephibosheth?

Psalm 145:13b

"The Lord is trustworthy in all he promises and faithful in all he does."

Broken and destitute, Mephibosheth was ushered into the king's palace where he received all the royal honors of a son. All because of a promise.

And that is our story, my friend.

We are the different... the needy. And because of promise, faith, and our Heavenly Father's inexhaustible grace, we have been seated at the King's table to feast forevermore.

Because—the truth is—there is no real difference.

DENYING DIFFERENCE

We learned from Romans 1:16 that salvation is for everyone who believes. But it was not always believed to be so. There was a bit of a learning curve with that truth.

Refer to Acts 10:28. Circle what was once deemed of the Gentiles by the Jews?

Holy
Family
Clean
Pure
Unclean

TouchPoint

"Neither Jews nor Gentiles have priority in how they are saved: both are saved by faith in Christ, not in any ethnic or religious distinctives."

John Piper

After Cornelius' baptism, Peter went back to Jerusalem to report the event (Acts 11:1-18). Acts 11:18 states what was finally realized. What did they learn the Gentiles could do?

Repent and receive life
Become Jewish
Join the synagogue
Remain separate

They were slowly beginning to realize that there was no difference between Gentile and Jew when it came to salvation in Christ Jesus.

Complete the truth taught by its Scripture:

Righteousness through_______________ Romans 3:22

He is God of the_____________________ Romans 3:29

There is_____________ _____________ Romans 10:12

That is our reality. But here—for our Greek woman—that was not yet the case.

How to bridge this divide, then?

That's our topic of focus for tomorrow.

TouchPoint

Judaizers, some early Jewish Christians, wanted to impose the adherence of Jewish Law upon Gentile converts to Christianity.

DAY 4

God, the Gardener

At the end of our cul-de-sac were trails through the woods and along the banks of a creek that the kids and I used to love to hike.

However, there was a point where we could go no further. The trail was divided in two by the creek, about 6 feet below. The divide was too far to jump, the creek was too deep to cross, and the banks were too steep to climb.

But we were determined to get to the other side.

It took several treks through the woods before the obstacle was overcome. We used some long boards to build us a bridge to span the ravine. One day we arrived to find our bridge sabotaged. The boards had been broken and tossed aside.

And so our work began on another plan.

Our next course of action was to pile up rocks in the creek bed to build a bridge of stepping stones upon which to cross over. This took considerably longer, but eventually we wore a path down the bank and made it across.

That lasted only until the rainy season when the floods came, washed away our rocks, and eroded our worn paths on the banks.

I've come to one conclusion. Bridge-building over a divide is not only hard work, it's temporary. And is often fraught with failure.

REUNIFICATION

Jesus came to bridge the great divide between God and man, heaven and earth. But what of the divide among men?

Jesus walked the soil of two camps: Jew and Gentile… us and them. There was to be no difference between them. We now know that Jesus is the Equalizer—removing that difference.

But what of the haves and the have-nots?

Before the Incarnation, you either had the promise or you didn't. Through a family bloodline, the promises of God were inherited down through the ages. But what if you were outside that family lineage?

God had a plan—and Jesus trusted it completely.

Galatians 3:28 tells us we are all one in

____

And Colossians 3:11 adds that Christ is in

____

Let's piece together other agents and means God used in the reunification process.

Ephesians 2:11-22 is an excellent passage that goes into great detail about what Jesus accomplished in reconciling the two camps.

- **Gentiles were brought near by the**

  ______________________ (vs 13)

- **Jesus reconciled the two groups into one by the**

  ______________________ (vs 16)

Ephesians 2:14

"For [Jesus] Himself is our peace, who has made the two groups one and has destroyed the barrier, the dividing wall of hostility."

Acts 1:8 informs us of two Agents used in the plan. Circle them:

Apostles
Pharisees
Prophets
Holy Spirit

TouchPoint

See Joel 2:28-29 to read the prophecy of the promised Spirit's coming.

Acts 22:21 reads: "Then the Lord said to me, 'Go; I will send you far away to the Gentiles.' " Who is the "me"?

In Luke 24:45-47, Jesus helped the apostles understand what, so that the gospel could be preached?

The use of the first apostles, with the later addition of Paul, and the Word—enabled and empowered by the Holy Spirit—would help spread the good news of salvation in Christ throughout the world.

There was another work done by the Master Gardener to resolve the separation issue.

THE GRAFTING SOLUTION

TouchPoint

Grafting: uniting the root and stem of one plant with the shoot of another, making them one.

Paul uses the analogy of grafting when writing of the method God used to merge the Gentiles back into the promise of restoration.

Read Romans 11:13-32.

Refer to verse 16 to complete the following:
If the root is holy, then__________________________ .

Check all that apply to what the grafted are commanded to do:

- ☐ **Do not consider themselves superior to the Jew**
- ☐ **Do not be arrogant**
- ☐ **But fear**
- ☐ **Continue in God's kindness**

TouchPoint

"Grace is given, not to make us proud, but to make us thankful. The law of faith excludes all boasting either of ourselves or against others."

Matthew Henry's Commentary

God's favor toward the Jews is from (vs 28)

____

God's favor toward the Gentiles is by standing in

____ **(vs 20).**

According to verses 30-32, both are recipients of

God's______________________________________ .

Paul is moved to close this chapter in the most beautiful words of praise. Read verses 33-36.

Are you of the grafted?

Jesus unites us all to Him, to the Father, and to one another.

He knew the time was coming for the Greek woman to no longer be excluded from His family.

And the time has now come for the rest of us.

Romans 11:36

"For from Him and through Him and for Him are all things. To him be the glory forever! Amen."

Spend a few minutes offering praise to God for mercifully grafting us back into His family.

___

___

___

DAY 5
Claim and Share

Well, my fellow sojourner, we have strolled the pathways of promise; crossed the ruins of barriers that once divided; and bowed in praise of Jesus, the Bridge-Builder who unites us all. Now let's return to the home in Tyre where a mother sought mercy for her little girl, and view the scene through the lens of Mark's Gospel.

Read Mark 7:24-30.

Who do you suppose the "children" represent?

What might the "dogs" refer to?

What can you imagine the "crumbs" as being?

What can you infer about her attitude? Does she appear to be

Proud
Tenacious
Humble
Witty
Bold
Distraught

If the feast was meant for the children of Israel, they could eat first. She would concede to crumbs ... scraps. But she wouldn't leave empty-handed. It wasn't that she was greedy or demanding. It wasn't that she wanted what belonged to another. And she wasn't asking for something for herself. She came seeking a blessing from the Jewish Messiah for one she loved.

A PROMISE IS A PROMISE

The myriad of problems resulting from man's sin from the fall in the Garden have been vanquished in Christ Jesus. We glanced at solutions God used to bring about our peace. He promised He would. And just as foretold, Jesus, our Prince of Peace, came to redeem, reconcile, and restore all things different unto God.

After all, a promise *is* a promise.

But Jesus mercifully blesses us beyond promise.

As He did this woman.

In her we see a prime example of the intercessory faith we explored last week. To seek God in faith and humility on behalf of another is to shoot straight through to God's heart.

And we can know this about His heart...

Acts 10:34-35

"Then Peter began to speak: 'I now realize how true it is that God does not show favoritism but accepts from every nation the one who fears him and does what is right.'"

Read Luke 11:10.

Who is it that finds God?

- ☐ **Everyone that seeks**
- ☐ **Everyone that knocks**
- ☐ **Everyone that asks**

How is the promise of God inherited, as mentioned in Hebrews 6:12?

____

Note from 1 Timothy 2:4 who God wants to be saved:

____ .

Our Father in heaven desires to gather all His children back into His family. So much so that His One and Only Beloved Son sacrificed His life in the most horrific way to make it possible. God sees us all as His.

And so should we.

What was Paul's charge to Timothy, as written in 1 Timothy 5:21?

Have you—though different—had the faith to come to Jesus pleading for mercy before others?

Did you, as our Greek woman, find it?

How might that change your view of the different?

Adversity has a way of bringing people to Jesus. And it was adversity that caused this woman to fall before Him, unashamed, and in full view of others. She boldly crossed barriers of race and religion to present her petition. Jesus tested the sincerity of her faith and she persisted. She was intent on receiving His blessing—as any mother would for her suffering child.

And the touch of Jesus?

He touched her with acceptance.

He touched her with His "Yes!"

Search the Scriptures for a promise of God He answered with a resounding "Yes!" in Jesus, His Son. Claim it for yourself. Your family. More importantly, be sure to share one that you have received with someone different.

Acts 2:39

"The promise is for you and your children and for all who are far off—for all whom the Lord our God will call."

Write the promise and the person here:

____

____

Give thanks to God with me that His grace is with us ***all***. And may we, the different, share that grace with all the different about us.

WEEK SEVEN

Would-Be Disciples, the Uncommitted

DAY 1

Shifting Tones

Week seven, and we're settling-in to the second half of our study. Don't get too comfortable, though.

This week will challenge and unsettle you.

As Jesus casts a glaring light on the hard truth of discipleship, His words will make us squirm.

He has a way of doing that, doesn't He?

NON-DESCRIPT DESCRIPTORS

Just for kicks, if I were to try a little exercise to match an adjective to a certain descriptor, it might look something like this:

Could-Be — **Procrastinator**
Should-Be — **Failure**
Would-Be — **Hopeful**

"Could-Be" has promise. "Should-Be" has regret. And "Would-Be?" This isn't the present tense sense like desiring or attempting. But past tense. Like, tried... and failed. But do you know what's worse? Having never tried at all.

Now pair that with "disciple."

"Would-Be Disciple"—talk about a contradiction in terms! That is the oxymoron of all oxymorons. Disciples cannot be "would-bes." You either are or you aren't. And when you are, you are NOW!

TouchPoint

Some antonyms for "would-be" are aspiring, endeavoring, striving, wannabe. Our "would-bes" are more along the lines of "would have been." They're those that would be if they chose to try.

SETTING THE STAGE

So far we have looked at people from whom we want to learn. People with characteristics to emulate. Not so with this profile! These are the conflicted. The people who want to move from following the world to following Jesus, but get stuck. All because they won't commit.

And we have seen the patience, compassion, and mercy of Jesus in healing and transforming lives. But now the tone seems to shift. And for good reason. Before we can plunge into identifying Jesus' touch, we have to set the stage. We have to see what is going on in the timing and background of the story.

Read Luke 9:21-36 and 51-56 to discover the What, Who, Where, When, and Why.

vs. 22 **What ...** did Jesus foretell?

____

vs. 30-31 **Who ...** spoke to Jesus about His "departure"?

____

vs. 51 **Where ...** is Jesus headed?

____

vs. 51 **When ...** What "time" is it?

____

vs. 53 **Why ...** were James and John angry?

____

The intricate combination of nouns and verbs in verse 51 explains an awful lot. Let's dissect it.

Underline the nouns and circle the verbs:

"As the time approached for Him to be taken up to heaven, Jesus resolutely set out for Jerusalem."

Look up the definition of "resolutely." Now list three synonyms of this powerful word.

1) ____

2) ____

3) ____

WHAT NEXT?!

The clock is ticking loudly in Jesus' ears as He nears Jerusalem—where the fulfillment of His coming awaits like a taunting bull's-eye. One can almost sense intensity building in the sequence of events in this chapter. Jesus had been trying to explain His imminent suffering and death to His disciples (much to their neglect); Moses and Elijah came to inform Him of His departure; the disciples have difficulties casting out demons; then He is not welcomed in Samaria.

All this leads up to this week's featured text.

Read Luke 9:57-62.

What do you detect in Jesus' tone?

The touch of Jesus is not always gentle, is it?

As His passion looms, urgency rises. Time does not allow for delay, indecision, or lack of commitment.

In the days ahead, we will unpack this passage to discern Jesus' touch more fully. But in closing today, won't you take the time to consider the following?

Has there been a time when you have delayed in following Jesus?

Have you ever made excuses for not being fully committed to Him?

TouchPoint

Jesus' definition of a disciple? Here is one from Luke 14:25-27: "Large crowds were traveling with Jesus, and turning to them He said: "If anyone comes to Me and does not hate father and mother, wife and children, brothers and sisters—yes, even their own life—such a person cannot be My disciple. And whoever does not carry their cross and follow Me cannot be My disciple."

DAY 2

Would-Be #1

I could share more stories about hasty decisions I made in my youth. Times I thought only of appearances and made foolish decisions. Times I thought rashly under high pressure. And times I recklessly didn't think at all.

Somewhere along the way I missed all the lessons on the value of prudence.

Ecclesiastes 5:1-2

"Guard your steps when you go to the house of God. Go near to listen rather than to offer the sacrifice of fools, who do not know that they do wrong. Do not be quick with your mouth, do not be hasty in your heart to utter anything before God. God is in heaven and you are on earth, so let your words be few."

Proverbs 19:2 states: "Desire without knowledge is not good—how much more will hasty feet miss the way!" Boy, did I ever miss the way! (And more than once.)

DISCIPLES = CALCULATORS

I can certainly identify with this Would-Be Disciple #1. I've made uninformed statements before counting the cost of my commitment. And when he did, Jesus met him with honesty.

Read Luke 9:57-62.

Complete what Man #1 said:

"I will follow you ______________________ you go."

Remembering from yesterday, where is it that Jesus is going? ______________________

This man was agreeable to following Jesus. But he was hastily agreeable. He was quick to agree to something he knew nothing about. And Jesus was quick to make it clear what was involved in following. Because if there is one thing about disciples, it's that they are calculators.

What does Jesus tell the man?

____

____

What do you think that means?

____

____

Following Jesus often requires sacrifice. It's not always comfortable or easy.

Jesus wants us to follow in faith. But He does not want us to follow in blind faith. He expects His disciples to make a calculated decision.

What does Jesus teach from Luke 14:28-30?

What are some practical ways to apply this principle to other areas of your daily living?

What plans might you be making right now that require you to count the cost?

What costs do you need to consider?

TouchPoint

"Jesus invited us, not to a picnic, but to a pilgrimage; not to a frolic, but to a fight. He offered us, not an excursion, but an execution. Our Savior said that we would have to be ready to die to self, sin, and the world."

Billy Graham

MISCALCULATING THE COST

We don't know what this Would-Be Disciple decided. But we do know of others in Scripture who miscalculated their options and chose to walk away from the promise of God—determining the cost to be too great.

Report your findings from Numbers 13:17-33.

How did the rich man in Luke 18:22-23 calculate the cost of following Jesus?

But we do know of others who counted the cost and said "Yes!" And we know the promise of our Lord to them, as well.

Following the same exchange between Jesus and the rich man, what did Jesus tell Peter about those who sacrificially follow Him, according to Luke 18:28-30?

- ☐ **They will receive much in this age**
- ☐ **They have done so without reward**
- ☐ **They will receive eternal life in the age to come**
- ☐ **They will be sadly disappointed**

TouchPoint

"Our Lord never pressed anyone to follow Him unconditionally; nor did He wish to be followed merely out of an impulse of enthusiasm."

Oswald Chambers

Jesus never forces anyone to follow Him. It always involves a choice, an informed choice. He has honestly given us our options; what to expect if we do or do not follow; and the conditions of following. He never glossed over the hard reality of what discipleship entails. But He has outmatched all that with the surpassing grace and enabling power of the Holy Spirit in our following.

The Would-Be Disciple #1 said he would follow Jesus wherever—before knowing that it may have meant following Him to a cross. We now know that for some, that is exactly what it cost them.

Do you think it's still worth it?

DAY 3

Would-Be #2

She was the princess of procrastination.

Little Miss had a gift for making excuses. And her standby argument worked for her, but mostly annoyed others.

When corrected by her mother: "You were told to_______________ (*fill in the blank*), young lady."

"Yeah-but," was invariably her quip.

"Yeah-but? Yeah-but, what?! Is that kin to a rabbit?"

Or her teacher might ask: "Did you do your homework?" "Yeah-but, I haven't finished it."

Unfortunately, this isn't some rare affliction reserved for little girls. This is a trait that's so ingrained in humans; it could likely be a link in our fleshly DNA.

TouchPoint

"Yeah-but"— it's an argument to placate; to appear to agree yet entirely disagree. It's used primarily to stall or excuse poor behavior.

ANOTHER WAY TO BE NON-COMMITTAL

Our Disciple #2 has his own way of dealing with Jesus. Two short verses can sure say a whole lot. Take a look…

What does Jesus issue in Luke 9:59?

- ☐ **An Invitation**
- ☐ **A Summons**
- ☐ **A Command**
- ☐ **All of the Above**

Circle the first word of the next sentence.

So

Then

Immediately

But

Fill in the blank to complete the man's reply:

"Lord,____________________ let me go and bury my father."

This seems like a legitimate request, doesn't it? On the surface, it would appear to be a noble gesture. Or is it?

"First let me…" puts a priority on things. "First let me…" can be the way of procrastination. "First let me…" just might be used as a guise for delayed obedience… non-commitment… misaligned priorities.

Does family take priority over obedience to following Jesus? (Consider Luke 14:26-27.)

Has there been a time when another allegiance has conflicted with your allegiance to Christ? If so, explain.

Matthew 6:24a

"No one can serve two masters."

According to what Jesus said recorded in Matthew 6:24, why is this problematic?

The potential to consider oneself a disciple of the teachings of Christianity yet never surrender to the Lordship of Jesus Christ is a real danger.

Jesus is to be the exclusive center of all of life. No exceptions. And His invitation to follow requires decisive commitment. Something this man was not willing to give.

PARABLES WERE MADE FOR THIS: TEACHING

Would-Be Disciple #1 taught us that discipleship outranks comfort and the familiar. Would-Be Disciple #2 teaches us that following Jesus supersedes family.

What else can we learn of priorities from the Master?

From Matthew 6:33 list the two things we should seek first:

1) ____

2) ____

What admirable attitudes are demonstrated in the parables found in Matthew 13:44-46?

- **Delayed reaction**
- **Immediately recognize value**
- **Decisive in responding**
- **Wait for a better time**
- **Willing to forsake all to obtain treasure**

Read the Parable of the Great Banquet in Luke 14:16-24.

Luke 14:15b

"Blessed is the one who will eat at the feast in the kingdom of God."

What word completes verse 18?

"But they all alike began to make ____________________."

- **Arrangements**
- **Excuses**
- **Changes**
- **Exceptions**

Match the verse to the priority given as an excuse for refusing the invitation:

Verse 18	**Relationships**
Verse 19	**Possessions**
Verse 20	**Work**

Have you ever struggled with putting one of these ahead of Jesus? How so?

What can you learn personally from these parables?

Excuses. They're just another means of avoiding commitment. Something Jesus desperately wants from us. Expects of us.

He knows well that when we prioritize possessions, career, or relationships above Him that we are setting ourselves up for a fall. For when these unstable things fail, then so goes the man.

He's asking the same question of you that He asked of this Would-Be Disciple.

Will you follow?

DAY 4

Would-Be #3

Just as Jesus **resolutely** set out for Jerusalem, He bids His disciples to fix their gaze straight ahead—ever moving *forward.*

He didn't look back to His quaint carpenter's shop. And He didn't look back to His family home in Nazareth.

No! He kept gaining ground *toward* what God had laid before Him. He was all in.

If only Would-Be Disciple #3 was!

NO TURNING BACK

When reading the response of Man #3 in this passage, we almost breathe a sigh of relief; "Finally! Finally, someone commits to following." Until we get to his next word. Words we're familiar with from Man #2 yesterday.

Note his first word in what he says next, in Luke 9:61

from the sidebar: ___ ___ ___

What is his second word?

___ ___ ___ ___ ___

And then he states he wants to

"go ___ ___ ___ ___ **."**

Luke 9:61

"But first let me go back and say goodbye to my family."

Here we have the classic "yeah-but" of our Little Miss; combined with rationalizing misaligned priorities; added to yet another Jesus no-no—desiring to go back.

"Back" may seem like a good idea when staring into the face of the unknown and fear raises his ugly head. But it isn't a faith-word, especially when God bids you "Go."

Look at Luke 9:61-62 again and thoughtfully consider the following:

What action causes trouble in plowing?

Has anything ever caused you to "look back"?

What might kindle a desire to "turn back"?

Has there been a time when you did look back and decide to turn back?

Is there something you need to turn from now to move forward, in faith, with Jesus?

Name someone you know who has gotten turned around that you can help move back toward Jesus:

WHICH WAY TO TURN

Scripture provides examples of those who looked back and those who didn't. I pray examining them will lend encouragement for whatever it is that you might be facing that has you asking which way to turn.

Hebrews 3:1a

"Therefore, holy brothers and sisters, who share in the heavenly calling, fix your thoughts on Jesus."

WHO	HOW	VERSE
______________	Looked back	Gen 19:23-28
______________	Wanted to go back	Num 14:2-3
______________	Strained forward	Php 3:13
______________	Run, fixed	Heb 12:1-2
______________	Looking forward	2 Pet 3:13

Here we see examples of both the committed and the uncommitted.

To be "fit for service in the kingdom of God" (Luke 9:62) is to be committed. And to be committed is to be all in. It's the equivalent of loving God with your whole heart, soul, mind and strength.

This Would-Be was met with the rebuking touch of Jesus. He would not accept a half-hearted reply. Because those concerned with things behind are often distracted and ineffective. Like Lot's wife, we can get so immobilized by things in our past that we can't move beyond them. We get stuck in the past with no hope of moving forward into the future Jesus has prepared for us. He longs for you to live a full and abundant life. And He knows you can't live that life by looking back and living in the past.

Paul applied an excellent choice of words, in that he was "straining forward." And sometimes, beloved, it requires just that: straining. In times of temptation and difficulty, it can be a taxing exertion to trudge onward. In those times look heavenward, where God has "raised us up with Christ and seated us with Him in the heavenly realms" (Eph 2:6). For therein lies our only deliverance.

DAY 5

Touching on Discipleship

I don't know about you, sister, but I sure have learned a lot from these three men this week. If I were to give a brief summary of the lessons learned from the account in Luke 9:57-62, it would look something like this:

Would-Be	Lesson	Touch of Jesus
# 1	Consider the cost	Honesty
# 2	Kingdom priorities	Correction
# 3	Serve straight ahead	Rebuke

THE DUALITY OF DISCIPLESHIP

TouchPoint

"A disciple was not only a pupil, but an adherent; hence they are spoken of as imitators of their teacher."

Vine's Complete Expository Dictionary

Discipleship—it's the gold coin with two sides.

On the one side, Jesus is calling us to discipleship.

On the other, He is commanding we go *make* disciples.

One calling bids "Come." To come sit at the feet of Jesus as a student. The other bids "Go." Go share what you learn.

Each calling has its own nuance; but both have the same expectation: commitment.

It is a total commitment, unlike our Would-Bes, that is without delay and without excuse. The precise level of commitment has been made quite clear for us in Scripture.

As previously stated, there are those who are followers of Jesus, but the mark of a true disciple is one who has surrendered to the Lordship of Jesus Christ and is obedient to the will of God.

Consider the clarification Jesus makes, as recorded in Matthew 7:21-23. What distinction does He make?

What does Jesus say in Luke 14:27?

What must a disciple be willing to give up from Luke 14:33?

What is the key to discipleship from Luke 9:23?

Is it a one-time thing when first you agree to follow? If not, then how often are disciples required to deny self?

TouchPoint

Arnéomai—to deny: "to disregard one's own interests."

Strong's Concordance

THE COUNTER-CULTURAL REVOLUTION

Much of Jesus' teachings was—and is—counter-cultural. They are hard teachings, no doubt. Upon hearing some of them, in fact, there were disciples who fell away (John 6:60-66).

However, Jesus made wonderful promises.

Note the promised result from each verse below:

Luke 6:40______________________________

____

Mark 13:13_____________________________

____

John 12:26_____________________________

____

The reluctance of these men was equivalent to unbelief. And the hearts of these Would-Bes were touch-less—because they refused the touch Jesus offered.

The touch of Jesus typically tugs at your heart and rouses a response unless you're more concerned with other things in this world.

And the touch of Jesus makes one commendable. These three fellows are now known to us only as the Would-Be Disciples. There's no mention of their names.

But look at Romans 16 and what do you see?

Names! There for all eternity are recorded names of the saints—committed disciples, each one.

We are called to be and make disciples. To receive the touch of Jesus in making us one and to share the touch of Jesus in extending that same invitation.

Let's make it our most fervent prayer to heed the call . . . and echo the call.

With whom can you share the touch of discipleship?

Discipleship is to share in Jesus' honesty about counting the cost; being committed to the point of sacrifice; denying self; and aligning our priorities.

It is good to regularly examine your priorities. Measure them to the standard of Matthew 6:33. Call it the 633 Rule.

Do your priorities conflict with your full commitment to Christ?

Ask yourself often: "Am I seeking first the kingdom of God and His righteousness?"

WEEK EIGHT
Bartimaeus, the Blind

DAY 1
Opening the Eyes of the Blind

He made his way, in the dark, to a spot just outside the city gate. He took his place among the beggars.

Same story—different day.

A commotion arose, and he could hear the rustling of a crowd abuzz with excitement.

"Who is it? What's going on?"

He could hardly believe the answer that reached his straining ears.

At the mention of His name, his faith saw what his dead eyes could not.

So, he took that one chance—in search of the merciful touch of the Son of David. He shouted out. For where his eyes could not lead him, his voice was sure to find the Messiah's heart.

Meet Bartimaeus.

TouchPoint

Bartimaeus, in Aramaic, means son of the unclean.

SEE WHAT ELSE IS GOING ON

Just prior to the Triumphal Entry, we have this profound encounter between Jesus and blind Bartimaeus.

Though it is recorded in the Gospels of Matthew, Mark, and Luke, we will spend most of our time this week in Mark's account.

Read Mark 10:46-52.

How many times does he cry out for mercy?

Once
Twice
Three times

Then what happened:

- **He was called**
- **Jesus kept on going**
- **He was ignored**

How did Bartimaeus respond?

- **He changed his mind**
- **He waited for Jesus to come to him**
- **He jumped up and went**

Write Jesus' reply from verse 51:

____

What is the touch of Jesus?

Immediately Bartimaeus ________________ AND

____ .

Bartimaeus receives the compassionate touch of Jesus in healing him of his physical blindness.

In Luke's account it states that he then followed Jesus, praising God, and leading others to also praise God (18:43).

Great story, right? End of lesson?

NO! There is a deeper lesson on these pages—one of spiritual blindness.

For that, we'll have to zoom out and go back.

THE BOOKENDS

God really opened my eyes as I studied this passage. And I am both honored and thrilled to share it with you.

He showed me new and wonderful things. Things I'd never seen before. He showed me the "bookends" to critical teachings of our Lord on His final journey up to Jerusalem. Mark frames crucial content with two similar accounts. A common theme threads its way through many of the exchanges made on this road trip to the end of Jesus' earthly ministry. There was something important Jesus wanted the Twelve to see and to understand. And it's placed between His healing of the blind.

That being said, let's now go back. Back to the first word.

Write the first word in Mark 10:46.

___ ___ ___ ___

Then—it's a word that points back like a beacon, shining light upon something relevant directly before.

Describe the scene in Mark 10:35-45.

____

____

____

What does Jesus ask in verse 36?

Sound familiar? Isn't that what He asked Bartimaeus, the blind?

And what does Jesus tell James and John in verse 38?

It seems they, too, might be blind about something. There seems to be more going on than meets the eye. So let's zoom out more to see if we can see the "bookends."

Look at Mark 8:22-26.

What is going on in Bethsaida?

Mark 8:22

"They came to Bethsaida, and some people brought a blind man and begged Jesus to touch him."

From verse 22 in the sidebar, we see people brought a blind man to Jesus and begged Him to

____

What does Jesus predict in Mark 8:31-33?

What does Jesus predict in Mark 9:30-32?

What does Jesus predict in Mark 10:32-34?

What happens next, from what we've already read in Mark 10:35ff?

And finally, what story follows, beginning in Mark 10:46?

Do you see the bookends yet?

What if you looked at this handy chart?

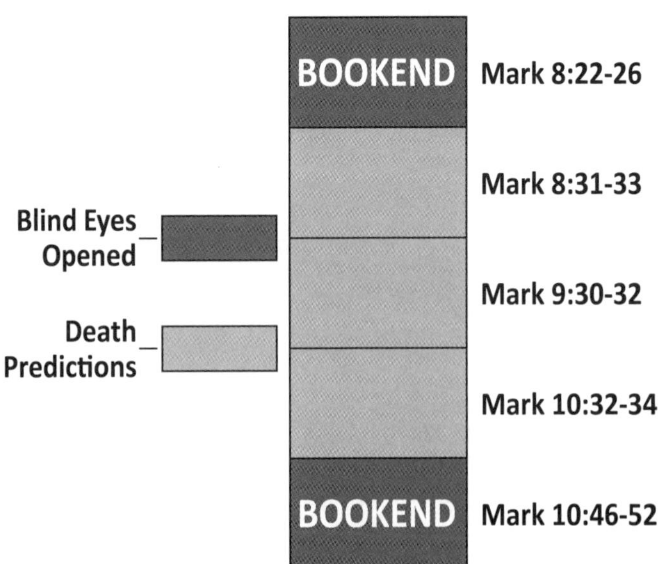

Jesus tirelessly tried to help those about Him see truth, but they seem to have been blind to it. And yet when He meets Bartimaeus, the Blind, He finds someone with spiritual insight.

Jesus called Bartimaeus to His side. Bartimaeus answered that call, and when Jesus opened his eyes, he followed Jesus—resulting in praise to God (Luke 8:43).

Jesus is asking, how will you answer:
"What do *you* want Me to do for *you*?"

DAY 2

Spiritual Blindness

She grew up in those pews. She practically sat in the same spot her entire childhood, but she never really got it.

So, when it came time for her to decide for herself, she just stopped going.

She didn't really see the value in it. And she certainly couldn't see the forest for all the trees!

As life groaned on, and she got bumped and bruised along the way, she thought she'd give it another go.

Sunday after Sunday she went. Nothing.

"What do people see in this church-business?"

But she was searching. She knew there was more to be found.

So she kept looking … longing.

Like Bartimaeus, she begged the Lord to open her eyes.

And one fine day, light shone through the gaping cracks of her hard and shattered heart, and she got a glimpse of the glorious grace of the most amazing Savior.

At long last, she could see!

TouchPoint

Vision—There is physical vision: when people saw the miracles of Jesus; and we can see the majesty of God in creation. And there is spiritual vision: like that of Ezekiel and Daniel; or of the Transfiguration and of heaven, as depicted by John in the Book of Revelation.

FAULTY VISION

Scripturally, blindness is a metaphor for being spiritually in the dark to God's truth. Let's look at a few folks who had vision, but just could not see.

Who could not recognize Jesus, as told in John 1:10?

____

After reading John 12:37-40, fill in the blanks.

Even after seeing______________ perform______________,
they didn't________________________.

Why couldn't they believe?____________________________

Where does this verse say understanding originates?____

John 7:3-5 tells us of another group that lacked the understanding to see and believe: Who were they?____

TouchPoint

Fanny Crosby, an incredibly gifted poet and hymnist, penned over 8,000 hymns. Through the eyes of a heart full of faith, she could see our Lord better than anyone with 20/20 vision. *Near the Cross* is but one example of her depth of spiritual insight.

"Jesus, keep me near the cross, there a precious fountain; free to all, a healing stream, flows from Calvary's mountain."

At this point, our scorecard of those that couldn't see was: the world, first-hand witnesses to Jesus' miracles, many of the Jewish people, and even His own brothers. Who else can we add to this growing list?

Who is the blind man in Acts 9:1-18? ___________________

What did he do when his eyes were finally opened?

____

Record the next word Jesus uses from the verses listed below:

Matthew 23:16—blind ________________________________

Matthew 23:17—blind ________________________________

Matthew 23:19—blind ________________________________

Matthew 23:24—blind ________________________________

Matthew 23:26—blind ________________________________

What tone is He using? And why?

What is His concern from Matthew 15:14?

Now we add to the list Saul of Tarsus (Jesus had to make him blind before he realized he couldn't see) and religious leaders of His day (if there's one group you want able to see, it's leaders).

Can you identify with any of these?

Has there been a time when you were blinded to a certain truth about Jesus?

Please realize that many of those whose eyes were opened, weren't able to see right away—like our woman. Why, even Bartimaeus had to first cry out... and then cry out more (Lk 18:38-39). Then he yet had to get up and go to Jesus.

If your vision seems a bit blurry, don't get discouraged. Keep seeking. Jesus promises to be found by those who seek Him (Jer 29:13). Remember that as we mature, our spiritual eyesight gets better and stronger (as opposed to our natural vision, which tends to get weaker).

TouchPoint

In answer to prayer (1 Kings 3:9), "God gave Solomon wisdom and very great insight, and a breadth of understanding as measureless as the sand on the seashore."

1 Kings 4:29

Read Proverbs 2:3-5. Match to complete the phrase:

Search	**As for silver**
Cry aloud	**Insight**
Look	**Understanding**
Call out	**As treasure**

Let's close our devotional time today praying the Lord open our eyes that we would have understanding and depth of insight—that we might see, follow, and praise Him all the more.

DAY 3
What Big Eyes They Had

There was an activity I loved to do with teens in Bible class. Without letting the students see the artwork beforehand, I would hold it close to their faces and ask them to guess what the picture was.

They could see all right! But only what was immediately before their eyes. (And even then they were wrong!)

It was impossible for them to see the bigger picture—no matter how good their eyesight.

None of us can truly see the bigger picture.

That is reserved for God... and God alone.

THE EYES HAVE IT

But there have been those who have gotten glimpses of sheer glory.

Starting in the Old Testament, and working our way up, let's look at those who were able to see the Lord.

Read Exodus 24:9-11.

Check all who went up to see God?

- ☐ **Moses**
- ☐ **Aaron**
- ☐ **Nadab**
- ☐ **Abihu**
- ☐ **70 elders**

What did they do in His presence?

Now read Psalm 63:1-8.

According to verse 1, what was David doing?

TouchPoint

Here are some quirky facts about eyesight:

- Normally, people blink over 27,000 times per day.
- With very little light at night, owls can see small animals from up to 150' away.
- Eyes process 36,000 bits of data per hour.
- Each eye of an ostrich weighs more than its own brain.

According to verse 2,

David______________ Him and_______________ His power and glory.

On rare occasions, God has revealed His glory to man—but never more so than the Incarnation. But even then, there were people who could not grasp His identity or His purpose. Their lack of understanding and disbelief were comparable to blindness.

And yet there were still others that didn't just see Jesus, they could see Who He Is.

TouchPoint

God used visions as a means of divine communication with prophets (as documented in the Old Testament). The New Testament records visions of apostles John, Peter, and Paul.

(*Acts 10:9; 16:9; 18:9; Revelation 9:17*)

Match the 5-W's of Luke 2:22-32 with its corresponding letter:

______	**Who**	**A) At the temple**
______	**What**	**B) By the Holy Spirit**
______	**Where**	**C) Saw Jesus**
______	**When**	**D) Simeon**
______	**Why**	**E) Jesus was a baby**

Simeon never heard a single sermon preached by Jesus, never witnessed one of His miracles or watched the compassion of God's Servant in action—and yet he had eyes to see the salvation of God embodied in that Babe.

Circle who was able to recognize Jesus from the account in Luke 4:41?

Disciples

Pharisees

Demons

Temple Priest

Who does John see Jesus as from the following verses?

- **John 1:29-30:**__________________________________
- **John 1:34:**____________________________________

And what did John do when he "saw" Jesus?

He wanted others to "see" Him, too!

Invariably, when you behold the glory of God in Christ Jesus, you can't help but point to Him in praise and draw others' eyes to His majesty.

Complete John 1:49:

Then_______________ declared, "_________________ ,

you are the___________ ; you are the________________ ."

And finally, Mark 15:39 mentions an unexpected man who saw Jesus for Who He Is. Note who that is:

____

TouchPoint

The existence of God is available to all men through *general revelation* (ex: Rm 1:20). God has broken through the natural order of things to reveal Himself through what is referred to as *special revelation.*

ex: 2 Cor 12:7

Yesterday we toured the Judean countryside, noting the spiritually blind along the way. Today we've set our sights on those that were able to have depth of insight.

Over the course of the next couple of days we will explore other scenarios and contributing factors to both conditions.

In closing today, however, meditate on what Jesus Himself said about those who will see God.

Write Matthew 5:8:

____

____

Examine the state of your heart. Is there an impurity that might be obstructing your view?

DAY 4

Seeing, Not Seeing, and Its Causes

I don't like cleaning windows.

I've come to the conclusion that it's an art form—it's either an area in which you're gifted ... or not!

I've also decided that I can only clean the sliding glass door to our patio in certain conditions.

If I make any attempt to clean it in the middle of the day, the glare of the sun is so bright I can't see the smears well enough. That, and the heat from the sun dries the cleaner so quickly that streaks soon appear.

When I try to clean it on an overcast day, the shadows make it hard to determine what's really there and what isn't.

But even on a clear day, I tend to leave smudges—and I can never tell whether they're on the inside or out.

I know I can't give-up in frustration. And I certainly can't ignore cleaning it. I've just had to learn how to clean them in the right light so I can see properly.

NOW YOU SEE ... NOW YOU DON'T

Light ... shadow ... disposition. The three of them seem to have an effect on my ability to see.

Sometimes I can see.

And sometimes I just can't!

When it comes to the changing ability to see the things of God for some of our Gospel heroes, I can relate!

Some had eyes wide-open. Some were blind as a bat. And then others could see one day ... but not the next.

Read these passages (just a few short verses apart) and note the following:

Verse	Who?	See? (Y / N)
Matt 16:15-16	____________	__________
Matt 16:21-23	____________	__________
Luke 24:13-16	____________	__________
Luke 24:30-32	____________	__________

Peter could see Jesus' identity, but not His purpose. And the Emmaus-bound travelers couldn't recognize Jesus at first but later could.

From John 1:35-36, answer the following:

Who is able to see?____________________________

How does he see Jesus?________________________

From John 1:38, answer the following:

Who is it?__________________________________

How do they see Jesus?________________________

Interesting! Why do you suppose John, the Baptist could see Jesus for who He is, but Andrew and John could not? The answer lies in John 1:32-34:

THE WHY'S OF SEEING

John could see because it was revealed to Him. And he has revealed to us the greatest explanation to the vision problem so many have experienced.

Find the reason in John 7:39.
What was not yet available to them?

____

Why?____

Psalm 146:8 tells us Who opens the eyes of the blind:

____

What is the source of revelation in

Matthew 16:17?______________________________________

All Three Persons of the Trinity help people to see.

The Bible also tells us of some other causes of blindness.

Match the cause with its corresponding verse:

John 10:24-26	**Darkness**
2 Cor 4:4	**Hatred**
1 John 2:11	**Not His**
1 John 2:11	**Satan**

GREATEST CAUSE OF ALL CAUSES

There are some real causes of spiritual blindness, as we have just seen. The greatest cause-of-all-causes is that of willful blindness (often inflicted by pride).

This particular cause was the instigation behind a major confrontation Jesus had with a group of Pharisees.

Read John 9:39-41.

John 9:39

Then Jesus told him, "I entered this world to render judgment—to give sight to the blind and to show those who think they see that they are blind."

NLT

After Jesus healed a man of his physical blindness (Jn 9:1-7), He sought him out to heal his spiritual blindness (Jn 9:35-38). Upon completing that restoration, Jesus used the opportunity to help some Pharisees clearly see their blindness and resulting consequence.

In this puzzling statement, Jesus plainly explains that He gives sight to those who know they can't see. And those that think they can are the ones that are blind... especially when it comes to sin.

When we see our sin and turn from it, Jesus can heal that. But for those who not only do not see it, but won't admit they can't see it, there is no forgiveness He can offer to them.

Jesus came into the world to bring salvation, but judgment to those that refuse salvation. If the Pharisees refused to recognize their blindness and were not willing to admit they were blind, they would never receive something they didn't think they needed. And they would be held accountable for that willful choice.

To paraphrase the essence of what Jesus is saying: "If you knew you were blind—and could see it—I would take it away. But you reject sight because you won't admit you can't see. Therefore, you will not be healed… but judged."

TouchPoint

Pray that it
never be said of us,
"You will be ever seeing
but never perceiving."
Matt 13:14

Until they would see that they couldn't see, they wouldn't see.

Willful spiritual blindness receives judgment. Period.

DAY 5

Setting Our Sights

Poor vision and blindness can be attributed to a variety of causes. It can result from accident or injury. It can develop gradually, from a hereditary disease; come on suddenly, due to an infection; or stem from other failing health conditions.

Some Pharisees attributed literal, physical blindness to sin, which Jesus addressed. And if a child was born blind, it was likely they would blame it on the sin of the child's parents, a subject Jesus also addressed.

We looked at some of the causes of spiritual blindness yesterday. It is with great praise and thanksgiving that we can now look to those things our gracious God has provided for our remedy.

Let's return to the story of Bartimaeus. What was his request from Matthew 20:33?

What did Jesus have for them?

What did Jesus do?

We are all beggars whose eyesight needs restoration. What comfort to know that Jesus looks upon us with compassion and is willing to bring about healing!

Can you remember a time He has healed your eyesight in a certain matter?

The healing of Christ for all mankind will be to restore our spiritual sight. So Jesus asks the question to the spiritually blind that he asked of Bartimaeus. A question you need ask yourself: "What do you want Jesus to do for you?"

Is there something you're asking Him for now in prayer—healing, resolution, blessing—when you should simply ask for *eyes* that *see*?

TREATMENT DIVINE

There are a few treatments to be applied to improve our poor condition—all of them spiritual in nature (since it's the spiritual that needs tending).

Paul interprets the gift of Jesus whom God has given to help restore us to see what He would have us to see. (And He not only resides in the heavenlies, but within each believer.)

Read 1 Corinthians 2:3-16.

By what means was the wisdom of God revealed to Paul (see verse 10)?

Verse 12 tells us what we have received and why:

Complete the teaching of verse 14: The person without the Spirit cannot ______________ or ______________ the things that come from God.

They consider them ______________________________ .

How are the things that come from the Spirit of God discerned?

The first thing God spoke into being at the beginning of creation was light. He knew that we would only see light by light.

Complete Psalm 36:9.

"In __________ ________ we ___________ __________ ."

John 12:46

"I have come into the world as a light, so that no one who believes in me should stay in darkness."

How do we stay in His light?

As daylight aids our physical sight, the light of His Son shines in our hearts that we may see spiritually.

So far we have established that to keep our spiritual eyesight healthy we must stay in tune with the Spirit and remain in the Light.

Matthew 6:22-23 lends insight.

What body-lamp do we need to keep healthy?

What happens when they are healthy?

What do you need to do to keep your lamp healthy?

Now let's look at Colossians 3:1-3 to help give direction in answering that question.

What are we to set on things above?

1) ______________________________

2) ______________________________

2 Corinthians 4:18

"So we fix our eyes not on what is seen, but on what is unseen, since what is seen is temporary, but what is unseen is eternal."

The New International Version translates "set your heart on things above," where the New American Standard Bible reads; "keep seeking things above."

Look to 2 Corinthians 4:18 in the sidebar to find *where* to fix the eye.

Why is that our focus?

To set our heart is to fix the eye.

Here's a self-eye exam you can conduct—and often.
Ask yourself:

Where are your eyes fixed?

Once our compassionate Lord has opened your eyes, can you see others sitting in darkness, needing to be un-blinded?

Compare the three translations of Mark 10:49 below.
Underline the disciples' comment in each:

ESV: **And Jesus stopped and said, "Call him." And they called the blind man, saying to him, "Take heart. Get up; he is calling you."**

NASB: **And Jesus stopped and said, "Call him here." So they called the blind man, saying to him, "Take courage, stand up! He is calling for you."**

NIV: **Jesus stopped and said, "Call him." So they called to the blind man, "Cheer up! On your feet! He's calling you."**

The disciples encouraged Bartimaeus and showed him that Jesus was calling. They helped him to his feet and then led the blind man to Jesus.

It can be phrased in several ways, using different words, but the message is the same. In gentleness and compassion, we can share insight into His Word and His heart that allows for Jesus to open spiritual eyes.

In faith, Bartimaeus cried out to Jesus; "I want to see" (Mk 10:51).

Do you want to see?

Time spent in the Light of the Son, in the presence of God, and in His Word will feed and fill the Spirit within you.

Know that Jesus has prayed to the Father that we might see His glory (John 17:24). Join the psalmist in praying; "Open my eyes that I may see wonderful things in Your law" (Psalm 119:18).

Fix your eyes and set your heart upon the eternal, that your eyes might be opened wide to all the abounding grace about us.

WEEK NINE

A Suffering Woman, the Hopeful

DAY 1

Within Reach

Sometimes, it's the suffering saints who preach the loudest sermon.

Their faith, their hope, their peace, and their resolve make greater impact than the most gifted speaker from the pulpit.

You've seen it, I'm sure. I know I have.

Time and again I've witnessed someone tame the dragon of adversity by the all-sufficient grace of God.

It's more than stoicism. It's more than forbearance. Far more.

It is undeniably genuine faith.

Name someone you know who has endured tremendous difficulties in a remarkable way.

Don't we need them? Doesn't their testimony (in words and actions) help us see the power of God at work in unthinkable situations?

Share how someone's testimony has inspired your faith.

THE POWER OF THE ALMIGHTY

Our profile-of-study this week is the nameless, suffering woman who reached to touch the hem of Jesus' garment.

(Fortunately, Jesus is never too far out of reach!)

Psalm 89:8

Who is like you, LORD God Almighty? You, LORD, are mighty, and your faithfulness surrounds you.

Jesus never touched this woman, but she was healed nonetheless, which is evidence of His far-reaching power.

Read Mark 5:24-34.

How long did this woman suffer?

Have you or someone you know endured a long-term illness? Explain.

Describe her experience seeking treatment, according to verse 26:

This poor woman tried everything. She exhausted every option available to her to no avail. Her affliction was incurable—in the hands of men.

And this disease—this hemorrhage she suffered—made her a social outcast.

What does Leviticus 15:25-27 say about a woman with her condition?

A woman with a discharge of blood was considered unclean. And anyone that would have come into contact with her would have also been deemed unclean. Therefore, she would have been ostracized socially, relationally, and religiously— likely left to suffer alone.

Whenever she was in public, she would have had to shout that she was "unclean." I have often wondered if the Pharisees had the afflicted announce "unclean" more as disgrace then warning. Though we must be willing to admit that we are "unclean" and confess that only Jesus can heal us, we are met with grace—versus *un*-grace.

Might this woman, who "suffered a great deal" for a long time, be considered desperate? Possibly. But one thing does seem obvious: she wasn't without hope. When she heard Jesus was coming near, hope sparked a mighty flame that sent her into the crowd.

So, in hope, she reached—acting on her faith in this Jesus.

Circle what she thought, as quoted in Mark 5:28:

If I scream, He might see me.

If I pay Him enough money, He might help.

If I could get His attention, He'll listen.

If I just touch His clothes, I will be healed.

If I'm lucky, He'll bring some relief.

Compare Luke 8:42b and Mark 5:24b and describe the crowd:

Jesus was touched by many in the crowd, but her touch was different. Hers was a touch of hope. And the faith contained in her touch released power to heal *instantly*.

Is there some "thorn in the flesh" (not just a physical ailment, but maybe something emotional, spiritual, or an unhealthy desire of the flesh) that has plagued you for a long time that you brought to Jesus for healing?

Search the depths of your soul to see if there might be something that you need to take to Jesus.

Learn these things from this precious woman to encourage your heart, dear one. You can't approach Jesus unnoticed (Lk 8:44). As He saw her (Mk 9:22), He sees you. He sees your need. He met her fear with a loving "Daughter" (Lk 8:48). Hear His whisper and do likewise—go in peace.

Luke 8:48

Then He said to her, "Daughter, your faith has healed you. Go in peace."

DAY 2

The Un-blessing of the Un-said

We've looked at several healings Jesus performed; no two are alike. Each is as different as the individual being healed.

Another conclusion I think we've reached is that the touch of Christ is always more than merely physical healing. And this week's profile is no exception!

When all hope seemed lost, at the realization that Jesus was coming, hope came alive, a hope that tossed her into a crushing crowd.

The woman was only one of many. Yet she was not lost in the crowd. Her hope set her apart from the crowd. And when she acted on her faith that Jesus could heal her, she captured His full attention.

The woman who wanted to go unnoticed was noticed by Jesus Himself.

Let's see if we can identify the touch that went beyond her healing.

PUTTING THE BLESSING INTO WORDS

Read of the encounter from Mark 5:24-34.

TouchPoint

Confession—as a verbal expression of faith—is to simply be honest with Jesus of our need and His sovereignty.

Check what happened when the suffering woman touched the hem of Jesus garment:

- ☐ **Nothing**
- ☐ **Immediately her bleeding stopped**
- ☐ **Jesus walked away**
- ☐ **She was freed from her suffering**
- ☐ **She went home unchanged**

From verse 32, circle what Jesus did after He realized power had gone out from Him:

He kept walking

He kept looking

He kept talking

Complete verse 33:

She_______________ Him the whole truth.

Jesus would not allow the blessing to escape unspoken. For a blessing left unsaid robs the blessing of becoming a *greater* blessing.

Read Luke 8:47.

From the account in Luke's Gospel, note the following:

- **In the____**
- **She told____**
- **And____**

It wasn't enough that she reached out in desperation, in hope, in faith—although that, coupled with His power, was enough to heal her.

CONFESS IT!

Jesus wanted more.

Jesus wanted her confession.

Jesus wanted her to admit publicly that He had healed her.

Faith should be expressed. It's not meant to be kept to oneself. It's one thing to believe in Jesus, but it's quite another to admit it.

We must be willing to testify before others of our desperate need of Him … our hope in Him. As well as what He has done for us.

Underline how the woman feels, as stated in Mark 5:33 below:

"Then the woman, knowing what had happened to her, came and fell at his feet and, trembling with fear, told him the whole truth."

Is it possible, considering her fear, that she expected to be met with condemnation or a harsh reprimand? But instead, she received commendation.

Jesus tenderly drew out the fruit of her lips.

TouchPoint

"*Homologia*" – a Greek noun defined as; "confession, by acknowledgment of the truth; derived from the verb "*homologeo*," meaning: to speak the same; agree; voice the same conclusion; assent; an agreement; a profession.

Vine's Complete Expository Dictionary

Often, it is our prideful independence that locks lips and stifles our confession. It also steals praise rightfully due God.

Her reach proclaimed loudly: "I need You, Lord. My hope is in You!"

And Jesus wanted her confession—a willingness to admit it before others.

Are you willing to confess what Jesus has done for you?

Jesus empowers the timid to testify. She was weak and too timid to ask for His blessing, but at His prompting she declared the truth.

Our confession brings refreshment and revival to us and others.

How often has someone else's confession lifted you up?

The blessing of Jesus was not just in her healing. Her healing was a vessel that carried multiple blessings. It blessed others in her confession. And it brought glory to Jesus in the presence of the crowd.

In the days ahead, we will more fully realize that confession is not only vital to our faith, but the faith of others.

DAY 3

Confession That Built a Church

We have much to confess!

What are a few things you can confess? Remember, confession is not all negative—we have more to confess than sin.

1) ______________________________

2) ______________________________

3) ______________________________

TouchPoint

Confess: to declare or acknowledge; to admit as true.

Confession can take many forms.

Name a few varieties of confession:

1) ______________________________

2) ______________________________

3) ______________________________

Confession can be made in joyful exuberance as worship. It can be a lament to God of pain or suffering. Or we can confess mournfully over sin.

Confession can be an emotional declaration of conviction; a matter-of-fact admittance of fault, ignorance, or wrongdoing. Or acknowledging God's transforming power at work in our lives.

We can boast thankfully in Jesus for our salvation; profess God's greatness; proclaim His goodness toward us. Or confess a benediction to bless our Holy God of Wonder.

Today, we'll look at the confessions of the ancients that build faith and helped to build a church.

CONFESSION—PAST, PRESENT, AND FUTURE

Are you ready to search sacred pages, down through the ages?

Let's examine a few confessors from the Old and New Testaments. The Bible also has a few words for the present and future about confessing the good name of our Lord.

What did the Lord say about why He raised up Pharaoh (Exodus 9:16)?

How did Moses make his confession regarding the Lord's deliverance (Exodus 15)?

Write the confession of Job in his suffering, as found in Job 42:2?

The Lord's renown would sweep the land as it was verbalized via confession—in all its forms. His Name would go before His people throughout the region, from generation to generation.

Match to complete the verses below:

The reward that awaits those that confess Jesus before others (Matt 10:32)	**Shout from the rooftop**
What the disciples were to do (Luke 9:2)	**God will also acknowledge them**
How the Twelve were to proclaim what Jesus whispered in their ear (Matt 10:27)	**Proclaim the kingdom**

From our Lord's own lips we have heard His instruction in this matter. Declaring what we know about Jesus is the calling of every Christian.

HEAR IT FROM THE CALLED

Peter had much to confess about the Christ of God. Though he denied Him (*and three times, at that!*), he spent a lifetime confessing the salvation of the risen Messiah.

What was Peter's confession recorded in Matthew 16:15-16?

Read just a portion of but one of his powerful sermons from Acts 3:11-16. What are a couple of the declarations he made of Jesus?

Paul was another apostle called and empowered to proclaim the gospel. God raised him up to declare the good news to the Gentiles and before rulers and authorities throughout the Middle East, Europe, and Asia.

What was his sole aim, as written in his letter to the Romans: chapter 15; verses 18-20?

Match the chapter from the Book of Acts with the ruler Paul testified before:

Acts 24	**King Agrippa**
Acts 25	**Governor Felix**
Acts 26	**Governor Festus**

Read Acts 28:30-31.

What did Paul do during the two years he waited in Rome for an audience before Caesar?

The apostle John writes that proclamation of what is known about Jesus brings about fellowship. There are other promises made about confession.

TouchPoint

Here's a sampling of different types of confession:

Praise
Thanksgiving
Admission
Benediction
Profession of Faith

Try one today.

What is the promise given to those who confess Jesus as the Son of God in 1 John 4:15?

Philippians 2:11 tells us what every tongue will confess: ____

Acts 4:20

"As for us, we cannot help speaking about what we have seen and heard."

It began with Jesus sending out the disciples with instructions to proclaim the kingdom of God (Luke 9:2). They built upon the foundation of the church with their good confession, and it has continued to grow and be strengthened with every confession since (see Acts 4:4).

God has consistently demonstrated the importance of the words we speak. For the words we speak can hold within them the life and light of the gospel.

DAY 4

Let's Be Honest

Confession is about honesty. Confession is about transparency. Confession is about Jesus.

Is it possible, that with our good confession, others can see straight through us directly to Him?

THE WAYS OF CONFESSION

Our woman was filled with the hope of healing. So much so that she dared to enter the crowd and reach out to touch the robe of this Man of Renown. But Jesus would not leave her there in her silence.

Her hope needed to be heard.

He moved her to give voice to her faith.

Can we share that same Jesus-touch with others?

Might we bring others to speak what is hidden in their heart?

Quite possibly.

But it begins with us. We must first exhibit what we want to see in others.

Knowing more about what the Bible has to say on the matter is the first step toward honestly confessing faith.

What did David confess in Psalm 32:5?

____

What was the result?

____

Psalm 35:28

My tongue will proclaim Your righteousness, your praises all day long.

Read 1 John 1:9 and answer the following:

- **What two things do we learn about God?**
    - o ______________________________
    - o ______________________________
- **What two things are promised when we choose to confess sin?**
    - o ______________________________
    - o ______________________________

What accompanied the Israelite's confession in Nehemiah 9:3?

____

In our developing snapshot, we learn that when we confess sin, God forgives—because He is faithful and just. Our confession should include our worship of the God who desires to purify us through and through.

Hebrews 4:14 encourages us to do two things:

___________ firmly onto and ___________ our faith

Circle *"profess"* and underline what it is we are to profess:

- **For it is with your heart that you believe and are justified, and it is with your mouth that you profess your faith and are saved. (Rm 10:10)**
- **Let us hold unswervingly to the hope we profess, for He who promised is faithful. (Heb 10:23)**
- **Through Jesus, therefore, let us continually offer to God a sacrifice of praise—the fruit of lips that openly profess his name. (Heb 13:15)**

From the verses above, we can add to the bigger picture of confession the aspect of professing our hope, our faith, and His wondrous name.

BRINGING OTHERS INTO THE PICTURE

Confession benefits us and blesses God. But confession has the power to bless others.

Our faith sees what God is doing in our lives, but putting it into words allows others to see it, too. And it turns the good deeds of God toward you into a blessing for someone else.

Meditate upon 2 Corinthians 9:13.

Circle what accompanied the Corinthian's confession of the gospel:

Contentment

Blessing

Obedience

Joy

Paul also commended them for their:

Good Deeds

Generosity in Sharing

Hard Work

Believing

TouchPoint

"Faith is confirmed by the heart, confessed by the tongue, and acted upon by the body."

Benjamin Franklin (Search Quotes)

Back up to verse 11. Their generosity resulted in

____

And in verse 12, we read that the service they performed would overflow in

____

The Corinthians confessed the gospel they believed and then acted upon that confession. Their obedience in giving prompted thanksgiving and praise to God, and their generosity would subsequently result in an abundance of many expressions to God.

Confession, accompanied by obedience, led to more confession.

So, let's be honest.

Let's be honest with ourselves … about ourselves.

Let's be honest about Him … what He has done and is doing in our lives.

That honesty keeps God in full view.

DAY 5

Contagious Confession

In these dog days of the advent of His return, our confession is more critical than ever in bringing blessing to the faith of others.

Honestly declaring the gracious acts of God is to lend courage in the face of trials; comfort for those who mourn; peace to quiet a raging storm; and proclaims the power of the Almighty for the weak and weary.

When our faith needs a boost and we're not hearing it from those about us, we can always turn to God's Word—it never fails us. There we can always find the confessions of those declaring God's glory and grace.

SONGS OF DECLARATION

The psalms are full of proclamations, declarations, and confessions about our God and His endless loving-kindness toward man. They have a great deal to teach us about confessing.

Psalm 19:1 in the sidebar tells us what of God's creation declares His glory?

- ____________________________
- ____________________________

Psalm 19:1

"The heavens declare the glory of God; the skies proclaim the work of his hands."

If the heavens declare God's glory, should we, His crowning-creation, do any less?

And if the skies proclaim His mastery, shouldn't the work of His hands proclaim the marvelous works of His hands?

What should we declare and to whom according to Psalm 22:22?

- ____________________________
- ____________________________

From the psalmist's confession, match what is declared with the verse:

Psalm 40:5	**God's Love**
Psalm 51:15	**God's Glory**
Psalm 71:18	**God's Deeds**
Psalm 89:2	**God's Power**
Psalm 96:3	**God's Praise**

Why is it necessary to declare anything at all?

Turn to 1 Peter 2:9. The text says that we are a

____________________________ people . . .

God's____,

that we may___________________________________

THE WOMAN WHO REACHED IN HOPE

Our woman came to Jesus with the hope of healing. She must have heard of His miracles and believed in His ability to heal.

How do you suppose that is?

Could it have been from the confessions circulating of what He had already done and was doing? And these confessions were contagious—spreading throughout the entire region.

That's the thing about declaring good news. It tends to plant seeds of hope. And the more you hear, the more hope grows.

Read her story one more time from Luke 8:42b-48.

She had hope for healing *before* her confession of what Jesus had done for her. What hope for healing did you have before your confession?

She had also hoped to go unnoticed. She may have been healed, but she didn't receive Jesus' blessing until *after* she was honest with Him about what He had done for her.

Confession is, first and foremost, God-honoring and God-glorifying. But then it becomes a blessing to its hearers.

The greatest confession ever made—and to be made even now—is "He is Risen!"

By that we are ever reminded that our Lord lives, is active in this world and is always near.

What does that confession mean to you?

What other confession can you make about Jesus?

Is there someone you can bless by sharing that confession today?

Psalm 34:3

"Glorify the LORD with me; let us exalt his name together."

WEEK TEN

Lazarus, the Bound

DAY 1

Raised and Freed

She came to me with a frown as big as Texas. And those eyes, speckled with gold, pooled with giant tears.

Tightly knotted in her little hand was a necklace—a treasured gift from her father.

She begged me to help her fix it.

My greater concern, however, was for that tender heart of hers, more tangled up in knots than the chain. It was heart-wrenching to see that child's mind bound with worry.

But because of its importance to my young daughter, I carefully worked those knots. As I did, I gently offered reassurance to unbind the knots in her and set her mind free from the worry that entangled it. As each knot loosened, she too became unbound from the fears that gripped her.

In the grand scheme of things, it may seem trivial now. But, at the time, it was significant to her. And because it mattered to her, it mattered to me. And because it caused her such misery, I was determined to put that smile back in her heart.

Because no one should be bound. Especially a friend of Jesus.

We have a long reading today. Read all the way through John 11:1-44. Then come back and answer the following questions.

TouchPoint

Lazarus is Greek, meaning "God helps."

Who was Lazarus?

From Verse 3, what was going on with him?

From Verse 5, how did Jesus feel about him?

Lazarus wasn't just any man, but a "certain man." More translations than not use the phrase "certain man" (see ESV, NASB, ISV, KJV, etc.). The Greek indefinite pronoun used here is "*tis*" (Strongs Concordance), which can be translated as "a certain someone" ... not just anyone.

TouchPoint

Lazarus, Martha, and Mary often hosted Jesus in their home in Bethany.

see Luke 10:38ff; John 12

You don't have to read the text long to get the clear impression that Lazarus was dearly loved by Jesus. This actually speaks more to relationship than just the fact that Jesus loved him.

Lazarus was a dear friend to Jesus. A friend who would bring glory to Jesus. A friend that Jesus would not only raise from the dead, but free from what bound him.

INTRICACIES OF JESUS ON DISPLAY

I sometimes think this is more of a telling story of Jesus than Lazarus. By it, we can see so many sides of Jesus. We get glimpses of both His deity and His humanity.

What feelings does Jesus experience? What emotions does He display?

How does Jesus respond to their weeping (verse 33)?

Jesus sees your every sorrow and is deeply moved by it. He can fully empathize with every human emotion.

Our merciful and approachable God became like us and has experienced our human condition ... our human suffering ... our pain and anguish, like no other. He can relate to how you're feeling about any given situation, because He has shared it and carried the burden of it to the cross.

When did Jesus weep?

Verse 36 states; "Then the Jews said;

____"

Verse 37 states; "____________ ____________________

of them said . . ."

How would you paraphrase these two verses?

Have you ever felt that way? "They say 'Jesus loves me', then why doesn't He____________________________ ?"

Read verse 4 and verse 15 again. Circle the reasons Jesus gave for not coming sooner:

Something else was more important
That they may believe
That God would be glorified
That the Son would be glorified

Jesus declared; "I am the Resurrection and the Life" (John 11:25).

When Life spoke, dead Lazarus arose.

I love the King James version of verse 44; "And he that was dead came forth, **bound** hand and foot with graveclothes: and his face was bound about with a napkin. Jesus saith unto them, "**Loose** him, and let him go"" (emphasis mine).

TouchPoint

The Saturday before the Crucifixion, Lazarus held a banquet in honor of his friend—Mary anointed Him for His own burial while Martha served (John 12). One week later, Jesus lay dead, bound in a borrowed tomb.

Lazarus was dead-cold and entombed ... until Jesus spoke life into him. But he was yet wound-up and bound-up tight. All the things the Lord despises ... especially regarding one He loves. So He said; "Unbind him" (ESV).

Are you aware of someone bound who could be set free by speaking of the life to be found in Christ? Name someone you can loosen.

We have much to uncover in the days ahead. But, in closing today, let's look at the result of the resurrection of Lazarus.

Match the verse with the outcome of the raising of Lazarus:

God was glorified	**John 11:45**
People believed	**John 12:10**
Death threat of Jesus	**John 11:40**
Death threat of Lazarus	**John 11:53**

Raising the Dead

She knew exactly Who to turn to ... where to go.

So she dispatched messengers to the Only Answer. Their Only Hope.

They waited.

He worsened.

The help they sought never came. "He ***will*** come," she anguished, as she peered down that long, empty road.

Time and again she caught herself nervously checking the horizon.
Time and again she caught herself reasoning her faith.

Overcome. Life's battle lost. They now waited for His comfort. "Surely He'll come to the funeral!"

And yet the day of their brother's entombment came—and went.

Their waiting continued.

Two days ... three days ... *four.*

They stared at that tomb without Jesus. Death seemed to have the final word—there, no greater mourning exists.

THE WALKING DEAD

TouchPoint

Lazarus was not the first dead person Jesus resurrected. He also raised Jairus' daughter (Matt 9:18-26) and the son of a Nain widow (Luke 7:11-15).

When the best time finally arrived, so did their Friend.

And in what could be the second most dramatic story in all of Scripture, we have a dead man *WALKING OUT* of his grave.

Re-read John 11:1-44 for a fresh look at the story.

What did Jesus know from verses 11-14?

____

But what else did He also know (see verse 4)?

____

How does Jesus feel about death (ref vs 33, 35, 38)?

____

Complete the "I AM" statement of John 11:25:

"I am the______________ and the____________________ .

Jesus not only stated that He is the Resurrection and the Life, but this miracle proves it.

Jesus knew His friend Lazarus was dead. And He knew He could and would raise him. He had healed others from a distance (Matt 8:5ff); He likely could raise the dead from a distance, as well. And I doubt it matters how many days, months, even years dead they may be, Jesus can still speak life into a corpse.

Same goes for the walking dead.

You know what I'm talking about—those whose faith has gone cold, all the life drained right out of it.

There is good news for them, too! Jesus has given the remedy for those whose faith has become lifeless.

Complete what was written to the church in Sardis from Revelation 3:1:

"You have a reputation of being______________________ ,

but you are____ ."

Verse 2 tells them to: "_______________ _______________!"

Verse 2 also tells them why they are dead. Circle the explanation:

You have completed the work.

You have reached your prime.

Your deeds are unfinished.

There is no more to be done.

Now look at James 2:17 and 2:26 in the sidebar and answer the following:

- **What does faith require to be alive?**

- **Complete verse 26:**

Faith without_______________ is__________________ .

James 2:17, 26

In the same way, faith by itself, if it is not accompanied by action, is dead.

As the body without the spirit is dead, so faith without deeds is dead.

Just as James wrote that faith is dead without deeds, Jude gave another insight in his epistle into the cause of those "twice dead."

From Jude 12 match other comparisons he made of the ungodly.

Clouds	**Without Fruit**
Blown	**Stars**
Wild	**Without Rain**
Trees	**By the Wind**
Wandering	**Waves**
Ungodly	**Twice Dead**

Has your faith ever gone cold?

If so, do you ask or mask? Do you honestly ask for prayer or additional help? Or do you put on a mask and try to hide it?

As we have already seen, Jesus weeps over His friends who have died. And He weeps over you when your faith has grown cold.

You can live a raised life... yes, even today!

PASSING FROM DEATH TO LIFE

Our glorious Lord revives the spiritually dead. And He raises those dead in their transgressions.

No one is bound beyond the power of Jesus Christ Almighty.

Just look at this amazing progression of death in these verses below!

Place the number that corresponds with the statement next to the verse (I did one as an example to help get you started).

1) Death enters world through sin	____	**Rom 6:5**
2) Wages of sin is death	____	**1 Cor 15:26**
3) Cross from death to life	____	**Rom 6:4**
4) Buried with Him, raised to new life	____	**Rom 5:12**
5) United in death, united in resurrection	3	**John 5:24**
6) Enemy of death defeated	____	**1 Cor 15:54**
7) Death swallowed in victory	____	**Rom 6:23**

Isaiah 26:19

Your dead shall live; their bodies shall rise. You who dwell in the dust, awake and sing for joy! For your dew is a dew of light, and the earth will give birth to the dead.

ESV

Death may be the enemy, but it will be defeated—swallowed up in victory! And just as Jesus spoke life into that 4-days dead-man Lazarus, He will speak new life into you.

Circle what pertains to *you* from Romans 8:11 below:

"And if the Spirit of Him who raised Jesus from the dead is living in you, He who raised Christ from the dead will also give life to your mortal bodies because of His Spirit who lives in you."

I have one last question for you today; and it was the question Jesus asked after He said that He is the Resurrection and the Life (Jn 11:25-26).

"The one who believes in Me will live, even though they die; and whoever lives by believing in Me will never die. *Do you believe this?*"

DAY 3

Tombside Teamwork

The design and intent in this study is to identify Jesus' touch upon those He encountered so that we can share that touch with those in need around us.

The primary touch of Jesus upon Lazarus is rather obvious here. And we also know that only He can raise the dead. But there is far more going on here, especially when we consider a "touch" as being something Jesus did that made an impression upon others to effect change. In that case, many people were "touched" by Jesus through the miraculous raising of Lazarus. In fact, people are still being touched by it.

Think about the onlookers in the crowd. Go back to the story (John 11:1-44) and envision the spectators. Try to put faces on the different people mentioned in the audience and list them.

Only a portion of two verses are listed below. Circle the pronouns in both parts provided:

vs 41 – "So they took away the stone."

vs 44 – "Jesus said to them,"

COLLABORATION OF THE "WONDER-FULL" KIND

TouchPoint

This divine collaboration is definitely more for our benefit. God certainly does not need our help (*we tend to create more havoc than help, to be sure*). But, in His great grace, God desires to bless us through the act of serving others in His name and for His glory.

There is a collaboration going on here... a collaboration of the ministry-kind.

There are some things only Jesus can do, like raise the dead.

But there are some things others can do in partnership with Him.

This collaboration is modeled in live-action for us in this account.

Starting in verse 3, what did the sisters do?

What did Jesus ask others to do in verse 39?

Did Jesus need help moving that stone?

What did Jesus ask others to do in verse 44?

Could Jesus have removed the bindings Himself?

Why do you suppose He asked others to assist?

What can be learned from this?

It all starts with prayer. Always. The sisters could not have begun with a more appropriate action. Prayer is something we can all do, regardless of our abilities (or lack, thereof) or the situation at hand. We can all, like the sisters, summon Jesus through prayer.

Once Jesus arrived on the scene He involved others. After He spoke new life into Lazarus, He invited others to "loose"—or minister to—the one He loved.

The greatest partnership He has called us to is that of sharing the gospel.

I think we can learn a lot about that collaboration from something Paul wrote to Philemon.

Let's dissect Philemon 6. Fill in the blanks from the word bank:

Share

Every good thing

For the sake of Christ

In the faith

Paul prays their "partnership____________________

__________________ ____________________

will be effective in deepening [their] understanding of

____________ _______________ ___________

we_____________ **for the**___________________

__________________ ____________________.

1 Thessalonians 3:2

"We sent Timothy, who is our brother and co-worker in God's service in spreading the gospel of Christ, to strengthen and encourage you in your faith"

From 1 Thessalonians 3:2 in the side bar, complete the following:

Timothy was a ____________________ in God's service.

For what three purposes mentioned?

1) ____

2) ____

3) ____

BINDING REMOVAL

Lazarus was free from death's hold, but he was still all wrapped up and unable to walk in newness of life.

To those standing by, Jesus commanded they remove what bound His friend.

No doubt, there are a number of things that bind Christians today.

There are those about us, for one reason or another, who have been raised to new life in Christ, but they're walking around bound up.

Is there anything that binds you from living in the freedom Jesus bought for you?

What mentor-in-Christ can you turn to for help in removing them?

What are some "grave clothes" people can get bound up in?

What can you do to aid in removing them?

Won't you close today praying for "the one Jesus loves"?

DAY 4

Instrumentality

We established from the text yesterday that Jesus involves others in the honor of blessing those He loves.

Quite often throughout history, God has privileged the flawed and fallen in the fulfillment of His plans.

Many are the plans and promises He has made. And He seems to take genuine delight in including us—as instruments in His masterful hands.

TouchPoint

Instrumentality: "The fact or function of serving some purpose."

Dictionary.com

"USE-FULL"—FULL OF USE

Jesus put to use those standing tomb-side. In awe and amazement they watched Him accomplish what would otherwise seem impossible. And He bestowed upon them the honor of being a part in His work that brought glory to God.

That extended invitation remains open to us.

What is your instrumentality? How likely are you to say "Yes!" to be used by God?

Is there something you have allowed Him to do through you?

Is there something now He can do through you to bless another?

You see, my friend, it's never a question of useful-ness, but willing-ness. Because God is perfectly and entirely able to do all things and fully equips and empowers the ordinary with grace sufficient for every task at-hand, we **are** useful.

The Bible provides an abundance of examples that we may see how God wants to use man as instruments.

First up? The apostles.

Read the account of the feeding of the 4,000 from Mark 8:1-10.

Circle the completion of the second sentence of the first verse:

Since they had nothing to eat,

Jesus called down food from heaven.

Jesus sent them home hungry.

Jesus called His disciples to Him.

Jesus told them to go eat and come back.

TouchPoint

There are so many outstanding stories in the Bible of ordinary people used by God to do extraordinary things.

Which one is *your* favorite?

Who did Jesus use to feed the multitude, as stated in verse 6?

Jesus was able to feed the multitude without any assistance, but He chose to use His disciples to bless the needy and feed the hungry.

In the account of Jesus feeding the 5,000, Jesus not only put the disciples to use, but included a boy's small contribution of his lunch in the gracious provision (John 6:9).

Next up? Ananias. (One of my personal favorites.)

Read Acts 9:10-19.

Write Ananias' response to the Lord's calling in verse 10:

____

From verse 11, Jesus used Ananias in answer to:

____

From verses 13-14, what was Ananias' concern?

From verse 15, why was Ananias to go?

From verse 17, "then Ananias______________________."

From verse 18, besides Paul regaining his sight, what was the greater blessing?

Two of the most powerful words are: "Yes, Lord!" By those words, Jesus has accomplished much.

We all have a purpose to serve in God's plan—that's our instrumentality. But we can't become instrumental—used as an instrument by God—until we give Him our surrendered "Yes!"

WHEN YOU'RE FEELING MORE INADEQUATE THAN INSTRUMENTAL

You may be wondering, "What do I have to offer?"

Well, we've already seen Jesus satisfy the multitudes with a boy's meager lunch (with an abundance of leftovers). And didn't He turn plain water into the choicest wine (John 2:1-11)? Set history ablaze using twelve ordinary men?

I get it. There are days when the ordinary seems all so overwhelming. Just look at Moses.

What was Moses' argument in Exodus 4:10?

What was God's comeback (see verse 11 in the sidebar)?

And what was God's promise in verse 12?

Exodus 4:11

Then the LORD said to him, "Who has made man's mouth? Who makes him mute, or deaf, or seeing, or blind? Is it not I, the LORD?"

ESV

Moses was not eloquent or quick of speech. He was an 80 year-old shepherd. True, he was chosen, saved by God as a babe, raised in Pharaoh's household. But he was a man passing common days in the fields of Midian.

You may ask the same questions of God.

Are you, too, feeling unable . . . unequipped . . . unqualified?

What truths about God's help you overcome anyway—regardless of how you may be feeling?

We may try to argue, excuse, put-off; but we are all use-full. And I am living proof!

This thing you're holding in your hands? These pages and pages filled with words? This is God at work. He is The One who makes me able. It is His sufficiency, His grace. It's not that I am useful, but use-full . . . willing to be full of use.

It starts with "Yes," then a determined commitment to be the instrument He enables you to be.

DAY 5

Fellowship in Ministry

The written Word of God has so blessed us this week in visiting the story of Jesus raising poor, dead Lazarus. We then noticed there was a collaboration of Jesus with others on-the-scene in ministering to His friend's needs.

Yesterday's journey had us looking at those God has used as instruments in blessing others—bringing us to our final stop this week.

TouchPoint

"*Diakoneo*" – a Greek word meaning minister or ministry. A servant's "loving action on behalf of a brother, sister, or neighbor. Jesus set both tone and example for Christian ministry"

Zondervan Encyclopedia of Bible Words.

And the Holy Spirit provides the gifts to serve the body in loving fellowship with Jesus. (*see Romans 12*)

A WHOLE LOT OF FELLOWSHIP GOIN' ON

The touch of Jesus is given to be shared.

In fact, the precise reason we are in Christ is for one another.

Read and complete Romans 12:5.

"in Christ we, though many, form____________________

body, and each member________________________

_______________________________________."

God showers us with love and blessing so that we can shower others with the same love and blessing we have received.

But our ministry to others must always be in fellowship with Jesus. He is to be the heart, motive, and Source of all we do in our servanthood.

In experiencing the various trials of this life, we receive comfort and strength from His grace—all the while realizing it is so that we can pass that comfort on.

That is established perfectly for us in one of Paul's letters to the Corinthians.

Read 2 Corinthians 1:1-7.

Paul praised God in verse 3 as:

The Father of__________________________

God of all_____________________________

TouchPoint

The body of Christ is more than fellowship in your local congregation. It is far more expansive than that. And yet, far more intimate than that, at the same time. On an intimate level, it is fellowship with Jesus and fellowship with one another within your church. But it is also a fellowship within the larger brotherhood, as members belonging to a universal body of Christ.

Activity 1—Match to complete from verse 4:

	so that they feel better
God comforts us	so that we can comfort others
	so that we can ignore others

Activity 2—Match to complete from verse 4:

	those that have it easy
In all our troubles	those with certain troubles
	those in any trouble

Activity 3—Pinpoint the source from verse 4:

Place the number to the corresponding word from the word bank in the blank that completes verse 5:

1) **Scarcely**
2) **Abundantly**
3) **Abounds**
4) **Barely**
5) **Limited**

"For just as we share__________ in the sufferings of Christ,

so also our comfort__________ through Christ."

From Verse 6:

If they are distressed or if they are comforted

it is for__________________________________ .

Circle to complete from Verse 7:

They share in both one-another's . . .

suffering and comfort

comfort only

suffering only

comfort and ease

BAROMETER FOR MOTIVE

There are eleven verses in the NIV translation of the New Testament teaching us to love one another.

To love is to serve. To serve is to minister. So then: to love is to minister.

But only in fellowship with Jesus.

Because just as Christ Jesus loved and served us in fellowship with God during His earthly ministry, we are to love and serve one another (see Eph 5:1-2).

And there are a few barometers we can use to test the motive of our hearts.

Read 1 John 4:7-8.

Loving begins and ends in fellowship with:

____

That is the beginning of ensuring the right heart-attitude—because the state of the heart is key. Ministry is not about the outward appearance. It is not about looking good. It's not done for show or to be noticed. It is a heart matter—precisely where God sets His gaze.

There was a man who wanted to be a part of the apostolic ministry. Read what Peter told him from Acts 8:21, in the sidebar.

What was not right before God?

____

Acts 8:21

"You have no part or share in this ministry, because your heart is not right before God."

Simon had impure motives, and they were able to see right through it! As does God. He searches our hearts to judge our motives.

We can also look to Jesus to see another good barometer for testing. (And an example can be found right there in our story of Lazarus.)

Read John 11:4.

Jesus—ministering in fellowship with God—was doing so for what purpose?

Do you remember when I told you earlier in the week that "Lazarus" meant "God helps"? Well, God helps us *to help others*. And Jesus has set us free so that we might be used in setting another free.

The Sovereign Lord Almighty can do all things for a sinner *alone*, but He has called us into fellowship with Him.

He could have rolled away that stone by Himself and He could have removed the wrappings by His very word (the same word that raised dead Lazarus). But He asks those around Him to participate.

What an honor and responsibility it is to be invited by Jesus to participate with Him in serving those in the Body that are bound by the troubles of this world.

With God, much loosing is possible—all to the glory of the Son!

WEEK ELEVEN

Malchus, the Wounded

DAY 1

Walking Wounded

The week ahead stretched out before him like a grueling Greek marathon.

The days of the Festival were quite possibly the hardest days of the year—especially for those serving at the Temple.

TouchPoint

How pivotal is this event? It's mentioned five times in all four Gospels.

Chaos, commotion, and crowds were bound to be a test in perseverance. With a die-hard commitment belonging to the youth of his age, he determined to serve the High Priest to the best of his abilities. So when the command came, he was eager to do his duty.

He followed this man, Judas, leading them. But behind him were an assortment of temple officials and a whole detachment of soldiers.

The short jaunt to the olive grove seemed pleasant enough; but then it all became a blur.

First a kiss, then words exchanged. Tensions flared in the dark, then a flash. In that one surreal moment, he groped for understanding—anything that made sense—only to find some sticky substance trickling down his neck.

But then ... ***peace***. Order instantly restored at the mere touch from the man he was sent to arrest.

Look over all of Luke 22 to get a sense of what is going on.

From Verse 2:

- **Who was "trying to get rid of Jesus"?**
- **Why?**

TouchPoint

The arrest warrant would have been issued by the Sanhedrin, and the arrest would have been made by the temple guards.

The crowd that descended upon the olive grove included a detachment (John 18:3), which was equivalent to 600 Roman soldiers.

Our main focus will be the arrest of Jesus. Just prior to that, where does the text say He was?

Read of the wounding of Malchus found in Luke 22:47-53.

How did Judas betray Jesus?

Have you ever known of someone who seemed to have friendly intentions, all the while intending to betray you? Explain.

Describe what happened next in verses 49-50?

Fill in the blanks from verse 50:

Struck the ____________ of the __________ ____________

Circle Jesus' response from verse 51:

He touched the man

He healed the man

He restored peace

None of the above

WHEN SECTS COLLIDE

Malchus was a servant to Caiaphas, the High Priest—injured by Peter, a servant of **the** High Priest, Jesus.

It's quite fascinating when you think about what these two represent. Malchus served the old priesthood that here clashed head-on with the new, up-and-coming priesthood. The temple authorities (the old church, if you will) vs. the new church (soon to be instituted).

One servant of God vs. another ... over Jesus.

In their zeal for the Lord, servants of God have been known to wound another because of Jesus. Are you familiar with any?

Have you ever had to endure an offense while serving the church body?

Do you know what I find even more amazing? Even though Malchus was leading the pack that came to arrest Jesus, Jesus healed him anyway.

The last person Jesus healed was the one injured on His account. He righted the wrong, redeeming the situation in that moment.

Read Matthew 26:52-54.

What did Jesus instruct Peter to do with his sword (verse 52)?

Whom did Jesus trust to defend Him (verse 53)?

Why was it important to allow the arrest to take place (verse 54)?

Peter, in his zeal and passion for Jesus, reacted impetuously to defend his Lord. Peter wanted to take control of the situation rather than trust that God was in control. Unfortunately, he haphazardly (albeit, naively) left walking wounded in his wake.

There are times when servants of the Lord get excited about a program or activity and charge in to take the reins, innocently stepping on toes in the process. Sometimes, those are the wounds hardest to heal.

As we wrestle with this topic this week, let's honestly go to God in prayer—examining our own actions and laying bare our hearts, that may just require the Master's healing touch.

TouchPoint

Each Gospel lends its own fascinating details.

Only Matthew mentions God's legions of angels.

Luke tells of the healing.

Only John mentions both servants' names: Malchus and Peter.

DAY 2

Words from the Wounded

Some scars you can't see. Because not all wounds bleed.

And not all wounds inflicted are at the hand of an enemy.

CAREFUL NOT TO REVERSE THE ROLES

No matter the gash, and no matter the offender, there is healing to be found.

Read Psalm 147:1-6 and fill in the blanks from verse 3:

The Lord____________________ the brokenhearted

and________________________ their wounds.

From Psalm 103:2-4 below, circle all the actions of the Lord:

> **Praise the Lord, my soul,**
> **and forget not all his benefits—**
> **who forgives all your sins and heals all your diseases,**
> **who redeems your life from the pit**
> **and crowns you with love and compassion,**

When pain has been inflicted, turn to the Lord for healing. He will heal every offense against His own committed in His Name.

Malchus not only was healed by Jesus, but defended by Him. And He is your defender, too. As He is to all those who suffer for the sake of righteousness.

Write what we are *not* to say from Proverbs 24:29:

____

____

Complete what the Lord said, as quoted in Hebrews 10:30, from the word bank?

I
The Lord
Mine

"It is________ to avenge;_____________ will repay,"

and again, "______________ will judge His people."

Also from Hebrews 10:30, what are *the Lord's* actions?

1) ____

2) ____

3) ____

TouchPoint

Who are some others wounded at the hand of another in the Bible? Just to name a few:

- Isaac, by conniving Laban (Gen 29:18-27)
- Joseph, by his own brothers (Gen 37:16-36)
- Moses, by his own countrymen (Exod 2:11-15)
- David, by a seething Saul (1 Sam 18:8-12)

It has been made clear that we are not to take revenge, but to trust God, for He is our Avenger. He is the just Judge that will redeem our hurts and reconcile all things (Col 1:20).

We must be careful not to reverse our roles. We must leave to God what is God's and release what is not ours.

AMPLE EXAMPLES

From Cain and Abel forward, the Bible provides ample examples of the wounded who have either been avenged by God or reconciled by His intervention. Let's see what we can glean from the story of Moses and Miriam.

Read Numbers 12:1-15

Who overheard the stabbing words of Aaron and Miriam

(verse 2)?____________________________________

Who defended Moses (verses 4-10)?_______________

What did Moses do in verse 13?

TouchPoint

You can read of the prayer and reconciliation of Job and his friends following their verbal attacks upon him in Job 42:7-11.

What was the final outcome?

Modeled for us is the prayer of Moses for his offender. God brought about healing and restoration to the disruptive situation.

The New Testament provides a few examples for us through some run-ins with the apostle Paul. There was the conflict with Peter (Gal 2:11-21) and the parting with Barnabas over John Mark (Acts 15:36-40). But we also learn of resolution and their reconciliation (1 Cor 9:6; 2 Tim 4:11).

We can learn much about the proper attitude to have in such situations from another classic example from Paul.

Read 2 Timothy 4:14-18. Match the sentences:

v14) The Lord will	**held against them**
v16) May it not be	**and gave me strength**
v17) The Lord stood at my side	**from every evil attack**
v18) The Lord will rescue me	**repay him**

Paul entrusted the situation with Alexander to God. Although he was abandoned by man, he knew God was always with him and that it was for the greater good of the gospel. Never looking back, he set his sights forward—to the Lord's ultimate deliverance into His heavenly kingdom.

Read 2 Thessalonians 1:4-7.

In all the persecutions and trials they endured, what was developed that Paul boasted about?

They would be counted________________________________

of the kingdom for which they were____________________

(verse 5).

Of what three things did he reassure them, from verses 6-7?

1) ____

2) ____

3) ____

You may not witness God's justice immediately. It may not come before the Lord's return, but we can share Paul's confidence that it will come (2 Thess 1:7).

There was no other more grievous injustice in all of history than the undeserved wounds inflicted upon our loving Savior.

He was despised. Wounded. Wronged. And yet He entrusted Himself to God—all the while forgiving His attackers.

It is by His stripes, stripes inflicted upon the sinless by the sinful, that we are healed. It was our sin—*my sin*—that wounded Him. That wounded the Father. And He endured those horrific, treacherous, and deadly wounds that we might be healed.

No wounds rival those. And there are none worse that cannot be healed.

Allow your wounds to be healed by His. Go to Him now with them. And leave them in His pierced hands.

TouchPoint

Pray with Jeremiah; "Heal me, Lord, and I will be healed."

Jer 17:14a

Forgiveness From the Forgiven

Recently baptized and full of passion for the church and zeal for the Lord, she got behind a ministry-of-interest and forged, full force, ahead. She wanted to learn the ropes, get involved; so she volunteered for every activity in the ministry. Not really knowing how things worked, she just followed her heart. Until it ran her dead-on a collision course with the seasoned leaders, set in their ways. Wounded by their indifference and cold shoulder, she retaliated with barbed words. Everyone retreated—limping away to lick their wounds—vowing never to expose or invest so much of their hearts ever again.

Sound familiar?

Though this story is fictional, it could have taken place in the Lord's Church, Anywhere USA.

THE NON-NEGOTIABLE

TouchPoint

A verb form of forgiveness used in the Greek is *charizomai* meaning "to bestow a favor unconditionally."

Vine's Complete Expository Dictionary

Wounds must be identified. Because unacknowledged wounds lurk in shadows ready to pounce onto the unsuspecting. They fester and boil and embitter the offended, holding them hostage, ever chained to the offense.

We must heal and move on. And the only balm for healing and key to set us in motion forward is forgiveness. It is a non-negotiable.

We can't talk about the wounded without following it up with a talk about forgiveness. For forgiveness is the next needed thing.

How important is forgiveness? How necessary? Let's turn to the only source to find such answers—Scripture.

Write Matthew 6:14:

____

____

____

Rephrase it in your own words:

____

____

____

Now write Matthew 6:15:

____

____

____

That pretty much clears that issue up, wouldn't you agree?

If only it were so easy!

But seriously, we must honestly look at ourselves and realize, like the servants in Matthew 18:21ff, that we all have debts we cannot repay. We are the forgiven, called upon to forgive.

Turn to the familiar prayer in Matthew 6. Read verses 9-13.

Is it possible to pray only half of verse 12?

Can we, the forgiven, expect to receive what we are not willing to give?

TouchPoint

"To be a Christian means to forgive the inexcusable, because God has forgiven the inexcusable in you."

C. S. Lewis

Read Colossians 3:12-15. Verse 13 says we are to "bear with each other and forgive one another." From verse 12, with what five virtues are we to clothe ourselves in order to do that?

1) ______________________________________

2) ______________________________________

3) ______________________________________

4) ______________________________________

5) ______________________________________

Verse 14 instructs us that over all these, we are to put on what virtue?______________________________

Complete verse 15:

As members of __________________ body you were called to ______________________________ .

The only attitude to have, so that forgiveness might be given, is that of Christ Jesus. And that is an attitude of humility, patience, meekness, kindness; and most of all: love.

AN OUNCE OF PREVENTION

Forgiveness is essential. However, it comes too late. For it comes after the offense, after damage has been done and the wounded lie bleeding-out.

Therefore, prevention is the best medicine.

The most damaging weapon in our arsenal, that tends to wound deepest and most often, is the sword of the tongue. And the Bible has almost as much to say about the tongue as it does forgiveness!

Proverbs 12:18 says

"the tongue of the ______________ brings ______________ ."

Proverbs 17:27 says that

the wise use words with ______________________________ .

Yes. It takes the attitude of Colossians 3 and a tamed tongue, but it mostly takes love.

The examples on both sides of our introductory story—post-wounding—required forgiveness. What could have been done before it reached that point? For that, let's turn once again to Paul.

Read 1 Corinthians 13:1-3.

Does it matter what gifts or talents I have, if I don't have love (verse 1)?

If I am the most spiritual person in my church but lack love, am I really anything at all (verse 2)?

If I give sacrificially or suffer willingly, do I gain anything if I do not love (verse 3)?

How many wounds can be healed by love? And how many spared?

I am ashamed to admit how many times I could have served with a more loving attitude, as opposed to just trying to "get the job done"—which is never the proper attitude in ministry.

Most unfortunately, wounding happens. We can still bring about healing. Even when we wound one another quite innocently, accidentally, or unknowingly.

From James 5:16 in the sidebar, complete the equation:

__________ ing + __________ ing = __________ ing

James 5:16a

"*Confess* your sins to each other and *pray* for each other so that you may be *healed.*" (emphasis mine)

Whether the offender or the offendee, we need to seek both healing and forgiveness—but complete healing cannot come without forgiveness.

How vital is it that we learn from the Master's words and ways to help prevent both?

DAY 4

Serving One Another in Love

Let's tip-toe back into the arrest scene in Gethsemane's garden and observe the interactions Jesus had with several key players in this event.

Note how Jesus deals with others in the verses below:

Person	Verse	Personal Note
Judas	Matt 26:50	
Malchus	Luke 22:51	
Peter	John 18:11	
Crowd	John 18:8-9	

Have you been in a similar situation as any of these (or maybe even all)? If so, what might you hear Jesus say to you?

TouchPoint

"But this has all taken place that the writings of the prophets might be fulfilled."

Jesus

How fascinating to see the way Jesus dealt with Judas, His betrayer; Malchus, His offender; and Peter, the rash. And notice how, when dealing with the crowd in John's account, Jesus put others before Himself—guarding what the Father had entrusted into His care, above personal threat to His own well-being.

Jesus' love for others never wanes—even in the face of personal peril.

Record what Jesus said to Peter from Matthew 26:52:

Jesus speaks to the essence of peacemaking here with the consistently proven principle that "you reap what you sow."

Swords are not the weapons of the people of Christ, but love. Our weapons are not of this world, but of heaven. And Jesus demonstrated that time and again.

Here, Jesus and Peter would part ways. They would not have occasion for any other discussions until after the Resurrection. And when Jesus reconciled the breach in their fellowship due to Peter's denials, He made His expectations clearly known.

Read John 21:15-17.

What does, "Feed My sheep" imply? What attitude did Jesus require Peter to have toward those who belong to Jesus?

Read what Peter wrote, as recorded in 1 Peter 4:8. Fill in the blanks to complete.

"_______________ ____________, ______________ each other_______________, because_________________ covers over a multitude of sins."

Peter, the shepherd of Jesus' sheep, experienced firsthand the covering of love. He had committed a "multitude of sins" and had them forgiven and covered by the perfect love of Jesus.

BODY PARTS

How do we avoid hurting others in our zeal to serve the Lord?

Read Galatians 5:13 and circle the answer:

Live free

Indulge yourself

Serve one another pridefully

Serve one another humbly in love

Let's expand upon the topic we broached yesterday: serving one another in love. That was the lesson Jesus had to impress upon Peter. And that was the lesson Peter learned the hard way.

Might a shift in perspective help us in this area? What if we didn't view our ministry efforts so possessively and other servants so enviously because we saw the bigger picture?

And guess who our go-to guy is on this one? You got it! Paul.

Read 1 Corinthians 12:4-14.

Different Gifts Different Services Different Work	} = **UNITY** = {	Spirit Jesus God

Identify the three "differents" from vs 4-6.

1) ______________________________

2) ______________________________

3) ______________________________

Note the Source of all three. Delete?

1) ______________________________

2) ______________________________

3) ______________________________

First, there are a variety of ways to serve—and all are needed. There are plenty of opportunities to go around to utilize all our contributions. Second, as there is perfect unity among the Trinity, there should be unity among the talents They generate.

From 1 Corinthians 12:7, what is the purpose?

____

Verses 8-10 list several "manifestations of the Spirit." And it expounds that all are needed. They are all given by one Spirit to each for the common good of the whole.

Circle the correct summary of verse 12:

Few parts form one body
Few parts form many bodies
Many parts form one body
Many parts form many bodies

Write verse 14:

____

____

Write verse 27:

____

____

This glorious body of Christ is not made up of 1—me—but of many. I am not the body, and the body is not me. But I have the honor to be a part of it with many gifted people—brought together in unity for the common good of the whole. We all have an **equal** concern—and when one suffers, we all suffer. When one rejoices, we all rejoice (1 Cor 12:25-26).

This chapter then closes out with the beautiful phrase: "I will show you the most excellent way" (1 Cor 12:31) and Paul segues flawlessly into the love chapter of 1 Corinthians 13.

No truer words have been spoken. Because love, undoubtedly and most assuredly, is **the *most*** excellent way.

And the most excellent way to serve, united in this one body of Christ, is in love. When it comes to love, there are just a few helpful tips to remember.

Read Ephesians 4:2.

What are the three key virtues needed in order to "bear with one another in love"?

Tomorrow we'll look more intently into cultivating these virtues. But, as we have seen today, when it comes to serving God's people in love, Jesus is our example; the Spirit makes it possible; and all are united in God.

One to Another

Let's amble down memory lane to revisit our travels this week.

We surveyed the wounded and healed amid the olive groves. We strolled the pages of Scripture for choice examples to follow. And we tried to come to terms with our own hurts; as well as those we may have caused along the way.

These aren't just any wounds, mind you. They weren't inflicted at the hand of enemy or foe. They likely weren't pre-calculated or planned. But the wounds we've explored are the ones incurred from other people of God, received by those zealously serving Jesus.

We hit the high road on the redeeming path of forgiveness. Our course then took a turn toward prevention. And to help keep from repeating an offense, we caught a fresh perspective from learning more about the body.

Along the way, our encouragement for the journey has been the faithful compassion and mercy of our Lord to heal.

Today we continue in the direction of servanthood, to contemplate more fully how to serve one another in love.

WOUNDLESS

Romans 15:7

"Accept one another, then, just as Christ accepted you, in order to bring praise to God."

So how do we keep our wounds to the bare minimum?
Or better yet: *woundless*! We must lean in close to hear God's voice coming up from worn Bible pages. The more time spent looking to the Bible for instruction, the more transformed we become to emulate the Living Word of God, Jesus Christ.

The New Testament is ripe with one-another passages. We could turn to any number or combination of selected readings on that topic. (And I had considered doing precisely that; but that would have had us jumping across as many as 16 readings.)

Really, only one is needed. The one "Biggie" tops the list.

Read John 13:34-35.
What is the command?

____

Instead of looking at a variety of readings on the subject, I selected one passage that contains enough instruction in this area to point us in the right direction. And, with application, will train us in loving servanthood.

Read Romans 12:3-21.

Paul begins with having the right opinion of ourselves.
How should we view ourselves (verse 3)?

____

____

____

Philippians 2:2-4

"Then make my joy complete by being like-minded, having the same love, being one in spirit and of one mind. Do nothing out of selfish ambition or vain conceit. Rather, in humility value others above yourselves, not looking to your own interests but each of you to the interests of the others."

Verse 10 gives us two "one-anothers:"

Be____________________ to one another

And_____________________ one another

What opinion are we to have of others (verse 10)?

Is it OK for us to be zealous in serving the Lord (verse 11)?

According to verse 14, circle how we are to treat those that persecute us.

Retaliate

Disfellowship

Bless

Curse

Complete the next three points from verse 16.

- **Live in _________________________ with one another**
- **Do not be _____________________________________**
- **Do not be _____________________________________**

According to verse 17, circle how we are to handle the evil that comes our way.

Repay evil

Avoid evil

Multiply evil

Do not repay evil

Fill in the blank from verse 18:

"as far as it depends on you, live at ___________________ with everyone."

What's the essential "do not" from verse 19?

____

Romans 14:19

"Let us therefore make every effort to do what leads to peace and to mutual edification."

From Romans 14:19 in the sidebar, what two things are we to strive for?

1) __________________________

2) __________________________

At what level of effort?

So we've learned not to serve the Lord with our swords. Or to be chopping off each other's ears. (*That doesn't make Jesus happy!*) But we have learned so much more than that. And by living what we have studied from Scripture, we will avoid hurting others in our passionate service in His Name.

In closing, won't you join me as I pray Romans 15:5-6 over you?

> **"May the God who gives endurance and encouragement give you the same attitude of mind toward each other that Christ Jesus had, so that with one mind and one voice you may glorify the God and Father of our Lord Jesus Christ." In Jesus' name, amen.**

WEEK TWELVE

Caiaphas and a Criminal, the Proud

DAY 1

Pride's Destruction

Let me just apologize in advance, ladies.

After spending a *whole* week in study about not wounding others in Christ, here I sit poised to inflict a little hurt.

And how do I know that?

Because in preparation of this week's study on pride, I *have* hurt (*conviction cuts deep*). I sometimes wince at the memory of lessons learned the hard way from this cancer-of-the-heart.

THE INESCAPABLE TOUCH OF JESUS

Twelve short weeks ago we stood in the temple courtyard with Anna and the newborn Baby Jesus. Now, we arrive near the end of His earthly life, to reflect upon final encounters.

We've witnessed many and varied touches of Jesus upon those He met face-to-face.

That is about to change.

You see, they all *wanted* Jesus' touch. They sought it. Welcomed it. Accepted it.

TouchPoint

Synonyms of pride: Arrogance, boastful, conceitedness, haughtiness, narcissism.

Antonym of pride: Humility

Our profiles-of-the-week this week did not. Because, you see, the proud refuse Jesus' touch. They see no need for it.

But you can't really call them "untouched." No one can come face-to-face with the Lord of Heaven and Earth and not be touched.

Even though they refused His grace, they were touched by Him. It may have been a touch of challenge or correction. Or maybe they were completely given over to their pride. But they were forever touched.

PAINTING A PORTRAIT OF PRIDE

Before any formal introductions are made, however, let's lay the basis for our topic this week. The proud will come barging in soon enough—as they always do. But for today, let's look at the characteristics and warnings laid out for us in God's Word on this weighty subject.

Read Isaiah's definition in Isaiah 5:21.

Fill in the blanks:

"__________ to those who are ________________ in their _______ eyes and _________ in their ___________ sight."

TouchPoint

Why is pride so much easier to recognize in others than in ourselves?

Look up the meaning of the word "woe" and record a brief description here:

Now it's one thing to be wise; but to be wise in your own eyes is only to be a fool. It is, however, a sure sign of pride!

A key word the prophet used here (and twice, at that!) is "own." A common problem with the proud always involves that three-letter word.

Another three-letter word to couple with "own" is the powerful word of warning: "Woe!"

Read Psalm 10:2-11.

Further describe the characterization portrayed in these verses.

Pride can often express itself in cruelty and mockery and even go so far as victimization, oppression, and down-right wickedness. Such a person, as clearly delineated in the text, does not seek the Lord; for "in all his thoughts there is no room for God" (verse 4).

When self has crowded out God, the proud are in grave danger.

To further paint this picture of the proud, turn to another prophet. Read Jeremiah 9:23-24.

Complete the "let nots" from verse 23:

Let not the __________ boast in his ________________

Let not the __________ boast in his ________________

Let not the __________ boast in his ________________

What can be boasted about (verse24)?

What is it the Lord delights in (verse24)?

Pride can come in many forms, as seen in Jeremiah 9:23. The Bible also depicts those with positional pride, possessional pride, intellectual pride, and spiritual pride. The greatest enemy to our Lord is that of spiritual pride—for then we are our own god. Having spiritual pride is polar-opposite to the humble and contrite heart the Lord desires of us.

NOTORIOUS PRIDE

If you were to compile a list of the prideful from the Old Testament, who would you include?

The most notorious that comes to mind is the Egyptian Pharaoh who ruled during the time of the plagues (Exod 4-14). Others in the spotlight are Samson (Judges 13-16), King Saul (1 Sam 9ff), and Nabal (1 Sam 25), to name a few.

The epitome of pride is found featured in two kings of Babylon, father and grandson: King Nebuchadnezzar and King Belshazzar.

Read Daniel 4:28-37.

Pride's dead giveaway is found in the king's boasting (verse 30). What pronoun did he use all- too-frequently?

What was his conclusion of the matter (verse 37)?

Now turn to the legacy he left by reading Daniel 5:18-31.

Where did the king's greatness originate (verse 18-19)?

What was the root of the grandson's problem (verse 22)?

What was the result of his pride?

Daniel 5:23

"But you did not honor the God who holds in His hand your life and all your ways."

King Belshazzar, in his pride, set himself against the Lord of heaven—a most dreadful place to be. In his arrogance, he misused the holy things of God for his own pleasure.

And that is precisely the destruction of pride—the high and holy things of God.

DAY 2

Priestly Pride

When last we left Jesus He had been arrested and was being led toward the Ancient City by a lynch mob. Ever the Peacemaker, He went willingly—trusting the Father's sovereignty and obedient to God's will. The evening was as black as the darkness that reigned, and the pride that ruled.

Through the midnight hours until Friday's first-breaking dawn, Jesus is volleyed about. He had to endure three mock trials before a Jewish audience: first Annas, then Caiaphas, and finally the Sanhedrin. He then withstood another set of three hearings before the Romans: first Pontius Pilate, then Herod Antipas, and finally Pilate, again. All the while, He suffered through their hatred, lies, and mockery; intermittent with the most cruel physical violence.

What can be said of the religious leaders of the day who planned, connived, and schemed to bring about an end to their perceived threat of the Man called Jesus? What can be learned from them? And what of the effect Jesus had upon them?

Fill in the "Who" blanks for the actions below:

TouchPoint

There were many illegalities in Jesus' trials. A few included:

- Held at night
- Conducted in the palace of the High Priest
- The accusation changed
- Did not follow proper trial procedure
- 2-3 witnesses in agreement were required

WHERE	WHAT	WHO
Matt 26:3-4	Plotted to arrest Jesus	______________
Matt 26:14-16	Bribed Judas	______________
Matt 26:57	Tried Jesus illegally	______________
Matt 27:1	Condemned Jesus	______________
Matt 27:2	Convinced Pilate to execute	______________
Matt 28:12	Had Pilate release Barabbas	______________
Matt 27:20	Had Pilate guard tomb	______________
Matt 27:62	Paid-off guards to lie	______________
Acts 4:5-7	Imprisoned Peter & John	______________
Acts 7:1	Tried Stephen	______________
Acts 7:54, 57-58	Stoned Stephen	______________

What can be deduced of them from what we've learned?____

____

____

To sum it up in one word? They were

____

WHEN THE PROUD GET PROUDER

The religious elite were educated, wealthy, and legalistic. There was a tendency to lean toward being politically minded, since the High Priest was appointed by Roman officials. Their own personal agenda was elevated above the righteous responsibility of the priesthood and excluded both God's will and the people's needs. To protect from potentially losing the power and prestige of their position, it was more advantageous to refuse to believe truth. And the undeniable miracles of Jesus they *admitted* were miraculous? They were not viewed as a blessing to others, or a sign of God, but as a costly threat.

They had so hardened their already-hard hearts that they would rather reject the Son of God than admit they were wrong about Him.

Are there people you can identify in the world around you who suffer from a similar trait?

"To some who were confident of their own righteousness and looked down on everyone else, Jesus told this parable:" (Luke 18:9)

Read Luke 18:9-14.

From verse 13, where did the tax collector set his gaze?

What was he willing to admit?

What did he seek?

TouchPoint

Caiaphas was both the High Priest and leader of the Sadducees.

The Pharisees tended to be more religiously minded. The Sadducees were more politically minded.

The Sanhedrin (which is the Greek word, meaning "council") was a type of high court for the Jews. The council of 71 members was made up of teachers of the law, elders, and chief priests.

TouchPoint

Caiaphas was the High Priest for 18 years (18-36 AD). His father-in-law, Annas, was the High Priest before him and was also involved in trying Jesus.

What attitude did he have that Jesus commended in verse 14?

What truth is declared in Psalm 147:6?

Caiaphas, the High Priest, squared off with The High Priest of God as the absolute antithesis of Jesus. He stared dead-on into what the priestly duties should have been about, but never was. What he could have been, but wasn't.

With each face-off, Jesus challenged and corrected him—which only made the proud even prouder.

TouchPoint

Caiaphas was deposed by Pilate's successor just a few short years after the crucifixion.

And when the proud get prouder, there's just nowhere else to go but down. Either down to your knees in humble repentance; take a tumble tripping over your own self; or cast down by the mighty hand of God.

Do you struggle with pride? If you were to rate it on a scale of 1 to 10, what would you consider your current level to be?

DAY 3

Criminally Minded

It's Friday, the 15th of Nisan.

And the end of His life is much like the whole of it.

He is confronted with belief and mockery. Wonder and scorn.

Here atop Golgotha's crest, pride and humility meet their Savior.

We witness the dueling of both dispositions as they collide at the cross.

Come to the cross with me as we look at the two touches remaining in our study.

TWO FINAL TOUCHES—LIFE AND DEATH

Judgment decreed, he now hung high on a hill in the glare of day. He recognized that he was just outside Jerusalem, near the main thoroughfare. And he took note of the two who hung to his left—companions in death. It didn't take long to assess the hostility that filled the scene, all directed toward the Man on the central cross.

Read Matthew 27:38-44.

What word is used to refer to the two crucified with Jesus, from verse 38?______________________________

"Mocking" and "hurling insults" indicate what attitude (verses 41, 44)?______________________________

Read Luke 23:32-43.

What word is used to refer to the two crucified with Jesus, from verse 32?______________________________

TouchPoint

The co-crucified are referred to as thieves and robbers in parallel Gospels. They are mentioned as rebels guilty of treason in other translations. We are not sure of their crimes . . . only their conviction.

Make note of the attitude on display:

Jesus—verse 34 ____________________

Luke 23:41

"We are punished justly, for we are getting what our deeds deserve. But this man has done nothing wrong."

Crowd—verse 35 ____________________

Soldiers—verse 36 ____________________

Criminal #1—verse 39 ____________________

Criminal #2—verses 40-41 ____________________

Criminal #2 to Jesus—verse 42 ____________________

Note the Jesus touch from verse 43: ____________________

Vile sin was unmasked and laid bare before Jesus. The Roman crucifixion was meant to shame, disgrace, and torture. But the insults? The mocking? Venomous pride coursed through veins to fuel these taunts. But Jesus still saw the desperate need of humanity. His compassionate mercy knew no end. It didn't stop. It didn't stop with the brutality or when the nails pierced His holy flesh or when that crossbar was hoisted heavenward. It never stopped short of His six hours in agony. It endured—to His final breath.

As did His humility. It did not cease in His suffering.

Does your humility know bounds? Are there triggers that cut it short; when pride's dragon raises its ugly head and kicks into high gear?

Pride's my poisonous bane! I have to constantly remind myself that "I have been crucified with Christ and I no longer live, but Christ lives in me" (Gal 2:20).

Two obvious attitudes in these two criminals—*two sinners*—blaze before us. They are reminiscent of two others in Israel's history. The last time pride and humility squared off so blatantly was in the days of Esther.

According to Esther 7:10, who hung from the gallows, losing his life as a result of his pride?

According to Esther 8:1-2, who bowed before the king to receive honor who was once decreed to die?

Haven't most of us stood on the other side of the cross?

Do you remember a time that you were the other criminal? Before your pride humbly surrendered to Jesus as Lord?

How did Jesus touch you at that crossing?

Has there been a time you crossed back? When you depended pridefully on your own good works or self-righteousness?

Your humble prayer to be touched once again is welcomed by graceful ears.

The three crosses stand to bring us to settle this heart issue with pride. They testify against us and hold up a sign pointing to God's solution—the salvation offered from the central cross of Christ.

Humble yourself and turn in faith to the Savior who hung there—buying your life with His.

Near the end of His life, Jesus touched many people in a variety of ways. Here we looked at but two—the touch of life and death.

In His own death, Jesus provided life for one humble, dying sinner.
And the other—the one filled with pride—refused His touch ... refused life.
That choice remained open to him right up until he breathed his last.
But scoffing was all the fruit his lips sputtered.

Romans 14:9

"For this very reason, Christ died and returned to life so that He might be the Lord of both the dead and the living."

I **cannot** close our time together today, precious one, leaving Jesus hanging on a cruel Roman cross.

No!

He lives! Our Savior lives! He has been raised in glory to touch our minds ... our hearts ... our lives. He lives to return some fine day—that we might be touched by His redeeming love ... changed forevermore.

DAY 4

More on Pride (*or should it be less?*)

Yesterday, the two criminals were placed side-by-side to contrast.

Today, we place Caiaphas and the criminal together for comparison's sake. Do you recognize their common, underlying attitude?

Underline the tell-tale words of pride of the criminal from Luke 23:39:

One of the criminals who hung there hurled insults at Jesus: "Aren't you the Messiah? Save yourself and us!"

Underline the tell-tale words of pride of the high priest from John 11:48:

"If we let him go on like this, everyone will believe in him, and then the Romans will come and take away both our temple and our nation."

ALLOWING THE BIBLE TO GUIDE PRIDE

Now turn to Psalm 34 and read verses 9-14.

Circle all the benefits of fearing the Lord and underline the instructions to heed:

"Fear the LORD, you his holy people, for those who fear him lack nothing. The lions may grow weak and hungry, but those who seek the LORD lack no good thing. Come, my children, listen to me; I will teach you the fear of the LORD. Whoever of you loves life and desires to see many good days, keep your tongue from evil and your lips from telling lies. Turn from evil and do good; seek peace and pursue it."

TouchPoint

"Pride is rebellion against God because it attributes to oneself the honor and glory due to God alone."

Holman Illustrated Bible Dictionary

What if Caiaphas and the criminal allowed those words to guide them?

What if we?

WISE WORDS ON PRIDE

The entire Bible is filled with many more helpful words regarding pride—especially the book of Proverbs.

Read Proverbs 15:33.

What is wisdom's instruction?

What comes before honor?

Match the proverb with pride's consequence:

Proverbs 11:2	**Pride leads to**	**destruction**
Proverbs 16:18	**Pride leads to**	**downfall**
Proverbs 18:12	**Pride leads to**	**disgrace**

These words of wisdom make for good warning of pride's destructive nature. We also learn from Proverbs that there are "six things the Lord hates, seven that are detestable to Him."

1 Peter 5:5

"All of you, clothe yourselves with humility toward one another, because, 'God opposes the proud but shows favor to the humble.'"

Which one tops the list from Proverbs 6:16-17?

How does God feel about the proud from 1 Peter 5:5 in the sidebar?

Jesus addressed not only the heart issue of pride, but its counterpart, humility (which will close out our week tomorrow).

Write Matthew 23:12

____

____

____

TouchPoint

"As long as you are proud you cannot know God. A proud man is always looking down on things and people: and, of course, as long as you are looking down you cannot see something that is above you."

C. S. Lewis

If I were to choose just one example of this verse being lived out, it would be 2 Chronicles 26:16.

Circle Uzziah's fate:

His pride gained him honor.
His pride led to his downfall.
His pride earned him respect.
His pride exalted him.

The sin of pride can stem from several sources. It can raise its ugly head from fear, jealousy, or for the sake of maintaining a certain type of appearance.

Jesus showed the better way of humility. He taught it and He lived it.

In His encounters with every imaginable personality type, we can see how He responded to people. We have seen His patience, His mercy, His grace, His forgiveness. But, when it comes to the proud, we see a different side of Him. A different demeanor.

He blessed the criminal who, in faith, simply asked; "Remember me."
He also granted the choice of the proud criminal to die a sinner's death without His saving touch.

As we learn from Jesus what *to do*, I think that it's just as important to learn what **not** to do.

And being proud is one of the biggest "Nots."

DAY 5

The Choice to be Made

As I tap this out on my trusty little laptop, I am overlooking a barn and a pasture (complete with horses), with the Blue Ridge mountains for a backdrop. I am on retreat with a group of fabulous ladies from my home congregation.

As I tried to come up with an intro for our last day on pride, I took a stroll across the grounds as the sun was rising. I soon came upon a barnyard filled with a number of animals. Right there before my eyes I saw it played out before me. There, on top of a shed, stood a goat, tall and proud as can be. But lying over in another area was a gentle llama, laid low to the ground, basking in the sunlight. The goat, trying to raise himself above the other barnyard animals, was in the chill of the shade, standing on the slippery slope of the roof. While the peaceful, gentle llama just lay content, in the warmth of heaven's light.

The proud and the humble.

And looking at the two, I came to the conclusion that if I were to choose, I would be the llama.

And it occurred to me that that's just what it comes down to—*a choice.*

I must ask myself the questions: "Is it more preferable to choose to be proud or humble? What choice would I rather make? Bow before Jesus as Lord or be my own foolish master?"

PRIDE'S REVERSAL

We read in Proverbs that the proud will tumble. However, when the proud do fall, we learn what happens next from Peter.

1 Peter 5:6

"Humble yourselves, therefore, under God's mighty hand, that he may lift you up in due time."

Read 1 Peter 5:6 in the sidebar.

What can we do when pride strikes?

What will God do?

Jesus taught of the attitudes and behaviors we are to have as His followers in what has been labeled the Sermon on the Mount. He preached of the blessedness of humility in what is known as the Beatitudes.

Read Matthew 5:1-12.

Circle the two references He makes to the humble:

Poor in spirit

Pure

Meek

Hungry

Persecuted

Proverbs 22:4

"Humility is the fear of the Lord; its wages are riches and honor and life."

Now match the blessing promised that goes with humility:

Poor in Spirit	**Inherit the earth**
Meek	**kingdom of heaven**

There is a unique blessedness, sister, in both heaven and earth for those who are humble. And that blessedness is the touch of Jesus upon your heart and soul. A touch given when the realization comes that we are destitute and then surrender our pride. The King grants entrance into His kingdom to those who come admitting their poverty, much like the beggars at the gates of old Jerusalem.

What does it mean to you to be poor in spirit?

What does Philippians 2:6-11 teach us on the matter?

Jesus demonstrated perfectly how to be poor in spirit. He chose to empty Himself of Self and surrender His own will to be obedient to God. He lived trusting God's sovereignty and turned to Him daily to provide for all His needs.

Just before Paul wrote about the example of the humility of Jesus Christ, he wrote about how we, too, can live lives of humility.

TouchPoint

The definition of the Greek word for humility has been translated by Joseph H. Thayer this way: "lowliness of human pride; that quality of mindset of having a humble opinion of oneself, i.e. a deep sense of one's littleness."

Thayer's Greek Lexicon

Read Philippians 2:1-5.

How do we live out humility according to these verses?

In what way can you apply this teaching to your life?

RIGHTFUL BOASTING

Being poor in spirit is not to live a life without joy. Passion. In fact, we are told that we do have something to boast about.

Read Psalm 44:8. In what may we boast?

Finally, from Romans 15:17, in what may we glory?

Jesus Christ—Son of the Living God, King of Kings and Lord of Lords, Creator and Sustainer of the cosmos—had every right and reason to boast.

He could have. But He *chose* not to. He chose the highest station ... a lowly, loving servant.

The same choice is ours.

What do I have in comparison, worthy of boasting?

Him!

And *only* Him.

Jesus, ever and always humble.

To paraphrase 2 Timothy 4:22, I pray the Lord be with your spirit and His grace be with you all as we share…

…the Jesus touch.

Conclusion—Remembering the Touched

Thank you, my fellow Bible student, for joining me on this walk with Jesus through the Gospels. We witnessed through Scripture those He touched along His journey to the cross. He touched the wounded and weary, the hungry and blind, the hope-full and the faith-full.

I don't know about you, but I'm not quite ready to close the cover and walk away just yet. I'd love one more look at those we've met. One more glance at those whose stories have made such a lasting impression upon us.

- There was Anna, the devoted. Jesus touched her spiritually by rewarding her faithfulness. She saw the fulfillment of God's promise after all her years of waiting. From her we learned to remain touchable ourselves and to touch others with encouragement in their waiting.

- John wanted to be reminded of the Messiah's identity as he sat unjustly imprisoned—persecuted for his undeniable faith. What he was feeling overpowered what he knew to believe. So Jesus touched him with much needed reassurance. We, too, can remind the weary that their suffering is worthy of the cause of Christ.

- Philip represented the practically minded. He taught us the patience of Jesus toward all types of personalities. We identified various traits and gifts within the Body and recognized that the touch of Jesus makes us all useful.

- Jesus ushered in an era of change, as was discovered with our next profile. Matthew experienced the transforming touch of Jesus. Jesus changed him from sinner to effective missionary. Filled with joy to be chosen and called by Jesus, he responded by celebrating his new life in Christ. What a lesson for us all! The touch we can share, as discovered through Matthew, is realizing the potential in others to be transformed by God.

- Jairus, the desperate parent, taught us to bring our children to Jesus in prayer for salvation. We saw Jesus' compassionate touch to heal his daughter and learned the greater lesson on faith. Our touch? Intercession, of course.

- The Greek Woman represented the different. She demonstrated courage to seek a blessing from Jesus on behalf of her family. Jesus tested her faith, and she passed. Ours is to realize that God's promises are for all people—regardless of difference.

- How blessed we were to see that Jesus' touch is not always gentle. Sometimes, when priorities are misaligned or we attempt to justify and excuse our poor choices, Jesus rebukes His would-be disciples. Through studying discipleship we learned that it is to be weighed carefully by counting the cost. But in the end, it is unquestionably worth it.

- Though Jesus opened the eyes of Bartimaeus, he had already demonstrated spiritual depth-of-insight. He had the faith to see Jesus for who He is, even though his eyes were blind. Meanwhile, the religious leaders (who should have been able to recognize Him) were the ones that couldn't see. When those around us lack understanding in a given situation or are too overwhelmed to see through eyes of faith, we can lend our spiritual eyesight to help guide them along those blurred paths.

- The Suffering Woman had faith enough to approach Jesus for healing, but she didn't have the voice to admit it. Jesus drew a confession from her that helped build the faith of those looking on. How might your confession of what Jesus has done for you bless another suffering soul?

- Jesus raised His dead friend, Lazarus. But He used others to unbind him to walk in newness of life. What a privilege we have to fellowship with Jesus in ministering to those bound by the woes of this world. We can be His instruments—working in collaboration with Him—to bring blessing to those dead-in-their-faith.

- By the zealous hand of the Lord's servant, poor Malchus, a servant of the High Priest, was wounded. He was injured all because of Jesus. But Jesus brought peace and healing to the situation. The valuable lesson we gained from him was one on forgiveness. We also explored how to best serve the Lord by serving one another... injury-free.

- We saw the pride of the religious leaders of Jesus' day and took note that the proud are the ones that reject Jesus' touch. Then we compared and contrasted the two criminals crucified on either side of Christ Jesus. We observed His interaction with them and posed the question of who we would rather be—because it does come down to a choice for us. We learned that being humble is to be like-minded to Jesus... and that inevitably touches others in significant ways.

They were all about as different from one another as different can be. And their needs were different, as well.

Is there one in particular with whom you most identify? Or maybe something Jesus said in their circumstance?

In every instance, His was a personal and unique touch upon those with the faith to believe.

Our Omniscient Lord knew each heart and each need then, just as He does now.

I pray that, somewhere along the way, you have discovered how He has touched ***you***.

Think now about those in your circle of influence. Is there someone you know with a similar disposition who would benefit from the touch of Jesus?

How could ***you*** be that touch?

Jesus, the enthroned and exalted King of Glory, reigns.

And He is still touching lives and loving lost and broken hearts.
By the grace of God, He has touched ours. And by that same grace may He use us to touch another.

Works Cited

- (n.d.). Retrieved from Bible Hub/Englishman's Concordance: http://biblehub.com/hebrew/bapperetz_6556.htm
- Chambers, O. (1992). *My Utmost For His Highest.* Oswald Chambers Publications.
- Franklin, B. (n.d.). Search Quotes. Retrieved February 13, 2014, from SearchQuotes.com: http://www.searchquotes.com/quotation/Faith_is_confirmed_by_the_heart,_confessed_b y_the_tongue,_and_acted_upon_by_the_body/13489/
- *Holman Illustrated Bible Dictionary.* (n.d.).
- Lewis, C. (n.d.). *Mere Christianity.*
- Maher, D. J. (2013, March 20). *Classifying Personality Types of People in the Bible.* Retrieved from Personality Cafe.com: http://personalitycafe.com/myers-briggs-forum/139813-classifying-personality-type-people-bible.html
- Murray, A. (1998). *Prayer Power.* Whitaker House.
- *Strong's Concordance.* (n.d.). Retrieved from Bible Hub: http://biblehub.com/greek/5100.htm
- *Strong's Concordance.* (n.d.). Retrieved from Bible Hub: http://biblehub.com/greek/4102.htm
- Tenney, M. C. (1985). New *Testament Survey.* Wm. B. Eerdmans Publishing Co.
- *Thayer's Greek Lexicon.* (n.d.).
- The *Westminster Collection of Christian Quotations.* (n.d.). Westminster John Knox Press.
- twentyonehundredproductions. (2013, June 13). *InterVarsity Christian Fellowship/USA.* Retrieved from http://2100.intervarsity.org/resources/myers-briggs-personality-types-bible-infographic
- (1984). In W. E. Vine, *Vine's Complete Expository Dictionary* (p. 120).
- *Zondervan Encyclopedia of Bible Words.* (n.d.).